101

IMPORTANT

WORDS

ABOUT

JESUS

THE REMARKABLE DIFFERENCE THEY MAKE

LEN WOODS

Our Daily Bread
Publishing™

Library of Congress Cataloging-in-Publication Data

Names: Woods, Len, author.
    Title: 101 important words about Jesus : and the remarkable difference they
    make / Len Woods.
Description: Grand Rapids, MI : Our Daily Bread Publishing, [2021] |
    Includes index. | Summary: "This book takes 101 words in Scripture
    surrounding Jesus and unpacks and demystifies them so you can clearly
    understand their intended meaning"-- Provided by publisher.
    Identifiers: LCCN 2020049001 | ISBN 9781640700826 (paperback)
Subjects: LCSH: Jesus Christ--Person and offices--Miscellanea.
Classification: LCC BT203 .W656 2021 | DDC 232--dc23
LC record available at https://lccn.loc.gov/2020049001

ISBN: 978-1-64070-082-6

Printed in the United States of America.

21 22 23 24 25 26 27 28 / 8 7 6 5 4 3 2

To Jesus the Christ,
Seeker of irreligious rebels
and self-righteous prigs,
Savior of screwups and lost causes,
deniers, deserters, and doubters

When I started high school, someone gave me a *Living Bible*.* Instantly, God's Word became more understandable. In college, I experienced a resurgence of my faith. In seminary, I took a few Hebrew and Greek courses and marveled at how rich and beautiful the very words of Scripture are. I began to see how the Bible really is "living and powerful" (Hebrews 4:12 NKJV). In the decades since, I have wrestled nonstop with the biggest question of all: What does it mean to take the words of God's Word to heart?

Given all that, how could I not attempt this project? I'm fascinated by the words of Jesus in the Gospels—and also by the things said *about* Him in the rest of the Bible. I'm also naïve enough (or crazy enough) to tackle really big topics. (For kicks, I just typed "Jesus" into the old Google and got just shy of two *billion* results!) So there you have it . . .

And here we go.

Before we begin our look at 101 important Jesus words (and their significance), do this: imagine a world *without* words.

(Tough to do since without words [a] I couldn't even suggest such an exercise, and [b] you'd have no way to think about, much less describe, your hypothetical, wordless world.)

Words are indispensable, central to our human existence. Words are how we label our thoughts, how we ascribe (and derive) meaning. It's only by using words that we're able to name our feelings, express our desires, and pass on vital information.

By stringing together various types of words—nouns and pronouns, verbs and adverbs,† adjectives and conjunctions, prepositions and interjections—we're able to form an endless number of sentences, have an infinite number of conversations.

Words are the lifeblood of human action and interaction. Teachers use them to help us think correctly; storytellers and

---

* An easy-to-read paraphrase of the Bible in modern English by Ken Taylor.
† Author Stephen King once quipped, "I believe the road to hell is paved with adverbs." Most writing instructors agree we should use them sparingly. But they are helpful (*sometimes*) in communication.

poets, to make us feel deeply; prophets and leaders, to point us in better directions and call us to better actions.

All these people know the great secret undergirding the universe: words are the deepest magic of all. They're dangerous and powerful, soul-killing and life-giving. Like nitroglycerin, words can blow everything up . . . or save the day. Stunning, isn't it? The same words that cracked open a hard heart today can be rearranged tomorrow to heal a heart that's broken.

A world without words? Inconceivable. Words are at the core of reality.

The Bible says this plainly. It tells us that the world we inhabit began with the Almighty . . . speaking words. Like a novelist creating a fictitious new world in which to set his characters and tell his tale, the opening sentences of Genesis show God bringing our real world into existence with nothing more, nothing less than words.

In time God selected some writers to help tell—using words[*] of course—the unfolding, unforgettable story of His world. How the characters He created in love engaged in a shocking mutiny, how a great curse fell over them and all creation, and how He immediately set in motion an epic plan to rescue and restore all things.

What a story! From an unlikely couple God brought forth a nation. From that nation came kings and prophets who used— what else?—*words* to speak of an even greater King and Prophet who would one day come and make everything right. The apostle John, one of the writers chosen to help tell this great story of God, even introduced this Savior as "the Word" (John 1:1).

---

[*] The New International Version of the Bible (the version cited most often in this book) contains just under 728,000 English words. Other (less concise) translations of the ancient Hebrew and Greek documents that comprise the Bible contain as many as 783,000 English words. All together, scholars claim the sixty-six books of the Old and New Testaments were written using a total of 14,000 unique Hebrew and Greek words.

• • •

A couple of Hebrew words are translated *virgin* in our English Bibles. The first refers technically to a young woman who has never had sexual intercourse (Genesis 24:16). The second word describes a young woman (who is sexually mature and who may or may not be sexually active—the question of her actual virginity can only be determined by the context).

In the oft-quoted Isaiah 7:14 prophecy about a virgin who would have a child named Immanuel, it's that second word that gets used. This was so that Isaiah's prophecy might have (a) an immediate fulfillment in the days of King Ahaz of Judah (a young woman of marriageable age becoming pregnant *as a sign to him*), and (b) ultimate fulfillment in the life of Mary, who "did not know a man." (This was a Jewish euphemism for sexual purity—and the literal translation of the phrase "since I am a virgin" in Luke 1:34.)

• • •

Interesting word meanings and ancient prophecies aside, the question remains: How, in the days before in vitro fertilization, could a virgin conceive a child? Gabriel explained the supernatural mechanics of Mary's pregnancy this way, "The Holy Spirit will come on you, and the power of the Most High will overshadow you. So the holy one to be born will be called the Son of God" (Luke 1:35).

And so it was that the child in Mary's womb had two distinct natures. He was the son of Mary *and* the Son of God, making Him fully human *and* fully divine.

• • •

Most moderns scoff at the Christian teaching of the virgin birth of Christ. But how else could an infinite Creator come into the world and fully identify with the plight of His finite creatures? How else could Jesus be fully God and fully human? Turns out that what seems biologically impossible was theologically necessary.

Besides, what better way to begin the world's most miraculous, mysterious story than with the wildest miracle and biggest mystery of all?

2

IMMANUEL

A proper Hebrew name that means "God is with us" (and that was applied to Jesus)

"The virgin will conceive and give birth to a son, and they will call him Immanuel" (WHICH MEANS "GOD WITH US"). (MATTHEW 1:23)

We would expect the first book of the New Testament to say a *lot* about the birth of Jesus.

It doesn't. Readers who want references to inns and swaddling clothes, mangers and shepherds will have to flip a few pages over to the gospel of Luke.*

Matthew focuses, instead, on an angelic visit to Joseph—the fiancé of Mary—to broach the subject of her surprise pregnancy (1:18–21). Then Matthew devotes part of one sentence—"she gave birth to a son" (1:25)—to Christ's actual arrival. From there he jumps to the beloved story of the Magi visiting Jesus—some days, weeks, possibly even years later (2:1–12).

Clearly Matthew was less concerned with the details of Christ's birth than he was its meaning.

• • •

---

* The gospel of Mark says nothing whatsoever about the birth of Jesus, and John's gospel speaks of it only in an abstract, theological way (see John 1:1, 14)

18

What *is* the meaning of the birth of Christ? How about the gospel announcement from Matthew above? In so many words he said, *Remember Isaiah's ancient prophesy about a virgin one day having a son who would be known as Immanuel? Great news, y'all! The birth of Jesus to Mary is what Isaiah was talking about!** (For those not conversant in Hebrew, Matthew added the explanation that the name Immanuel means "God with us.")

Since we have no record of anyone ever calling Mary's son *Immanuel*,† it seems *Immanuel* is meant to be more a description of who and what He was than an actual name.

● ● ●

The phrase is stunning no matter how you say it: *God* with us. God *with* us. God with *us*.

Goodness gracious, the implications of the truth we celebrate each Christmas! If we close our eyes, we can see Him still—the infinite infant. Deity in diapers. The One who made the heavens and sits enthroned above them, curled up in an animal feeding trough. Each December, we wonder at the God who showed up, the God who plopped down in our midst!

(If thoughts like these don't make your head swim and your heart race—at least a little bit—maybe you should have a friend in the medical field check your vital signs.)

● ● ●

Immanuel means God isn't aloof and remote. He took on human form and came and lived among us (John 1:1, 14). And for those

---

* Unless he was from the southern part of Israel, it's doubtful that Matthew said *y'all*, though that is clearly what he meant.

† Matthew wrote that the angel told Joseph "to give him the name Jesus, because he will save his people from their sins" (1:21).

of us who are believers, it's even better: He's not simply God *with* us, He is also God *in* us (see Colossians 1:27).

Immanuel means something else—that everything will likely get crazy before all ends well. Mary and Joseph were going about their business, planning a wedding and dreaming about a future together when God came barging into their lives, disrupting everything.

But notice their humble response. They embraced Immanuel. They surrendered their wills, laid down their plans, and welcomed Him into their lives. "Okay," they essentially gulped, "here we go. No doubt this is going to be a wild ride, but at the very least God will—literally—be with us."

It's a selfless attitude like theirs that allows us to be part of wonderful and eternal things.

3

BORN

The natural process by which humans enter the world

While they were there, the time came for the baby to be born, and she gave birth to her firstborn, a son. (LUKE 2:6–7)

Since Luke's credentials included "medical doctor" (Colossians 4:14) and "meticulous investigator" (Luke 1:1–4), we can't help wondering, *Why didn't He provide a few more details about the coming of Christ into the world?*

We have so many questions: Did it happen in a stable or a cave? Were animals present (like they are in our modern-day nativity sets)? How long was Mary's labor? Did Joseph pace back and forth like most first-time fathers? Was it just the two of them all alone in the night? How much did the baby weigh? How loudly did He cry?

If Luke knew all this information, he didn't divulge it. He only reported that "while they were there"—in Bethlehem—the baby was *born*. Mary "gave birth to . . . a son."

• • •

I've been in the room for two births (three, if I count the one I was too young to remember). At the most basic level, birth is the

4

ANGEL

Spirit beings created to serve God and do His bidding

An angel of the Lord appeared to them, and the glory of the Lord shone
around them, and they were terrified. (LUKE 2:9)

Most people prefer *adorable* angels (like Raphael's famous
cherub babies) or *endearing* ones (like the lovable Clarence
in the classic holiday movie *It's a Wonderful Life*). They see such
depictions and murmur, *Aww!*

The angels of the Bible elicit a different sort of awe. When they
show up, they invariably feel the need to blurt out disclaimers
along the lines of, "Don't stroke out. You're going to be okay." Even
then, divine messengers often leave people hyperventilating
or speechless or trembling or face down . . . sometimes all of
the above.

Here's another true thing: Every time angels show up in the
great story of God, it means things are about to get interesting.
And one final important fact: Just before and just after the birth
of Christ, angels were popping up *everywhere*.

• • •

The word *angel* literally means "messenger" or "one dispatched
to deliver news." Prior to the birth of Christ, an angel identified
as Gabriel appeared to Zechariah the priest to let him know that

he and his wife, Elizabeth, were going to have a son who would prepare Israel for the coming of the Lord (Luke 1:11–19). Not long after that, as we've mentioned, Gabriel appeared to Mary (Luke 1:30–35) to inform her that she—as a virgin—would become pregnant with the Son of God. Joseph—her confused fiancé—got an angelic visit and explanation too (Matthew 1:18–25).

On the day Mary's child—God's Son—was born, the angels of God were working overtime. One relayed the good news of Christ's birth to an anonymous group of shepherds in the fields outside Bethlehem. Luke tells us that before these terrified men could even process such a staggering announcement, this angel was joined by "a great company of the heavenly host" (Luke 2:13).

In other words, a vast angelic army filled the skies above the little town of Bethlehem. Why? Because earth was being invaded by heaven. Liberation was at hand. The forces of righteousness were martialing for a decisive campaign against evil.

●   ●   ●

A surprising number of Christians think it's possible for them to become angels when they die. That if they play their cards—live their lives—just right, they can "earn their wings." It's a fascinating thought; however, nothing in the Bible supports this idea.

Humans don't become angels—although, when we share the news of the coming of Christ, we *are* being "angelic" in the most literal sense of the word.

●   ●   ●

What good is a heavenly message if we don't heed it? Hear again the stunning news announced by the angel of Christmas: "Do not be afraid. I bring you good news that will cause great joy for all the people. Today in the town of David a Savior has been born to you; he is the Messiah, the Lord" (Luke 2:10–11).

5

SAVIOR

One who rescues or delivers others from physical
or spiritual trouble

Today in the town of David a Savior has been born to you;
he is the Messiah, the Lord. (LUKE 2:11)

The angel hovering overhead could have said, "A *child* has been born" (or "a bouncing baby boy" or "a handsome little guy" or "a future carpenter—you should see the size of that kid's hands"). He didn't choose any of those words.

Instead, he told the gob-smacked shepherds about the arrival of a "Savior."

• • •

Our culture knows a little something about saving things. We save dates, seats, and room. Often we find ourselves trying to save time or money or face.

So what's a *savior*? It's one who *saves*, one who brings *salvation*. A *savior* is a rescuer or deliverer. We might say that a savior saves another's neck or skin—which is a way of saying, saves one's life.

People of faith hear this family of words and immediately think primarily in spiritual and eternal terms—being saved (forgiven) *by God* and thus spared the unthinkable fate of separation from Him forever. That *is* salvation in the ultimate sense. It's why God sent His Son (John 3:17). It's why Jesus came (Luke 19:10).

But the word *Savior*—if you can believe it—means even more than that.

• • •

There's no telling what personal struggles those startled shepherds[*] faced. Shame? Crushing guilt? Heavy regret? Crippling fear . . . or insecurity? Depression, perhaps? Envy? Bitterness? A pessimistic outlook on life, maybe? Some sort of compulsive behavior? A bad temper? A destructive habit? God only knows what things they needed to be rescued from.

It's a safe bet that when they showed up at Mary's makeshift maternity ward, the proud new father whispered, "We named him Jesus" (Matthew 1:21).

Perfect.

Of course.

The name *Jesus* means "the Lord saves."

• • •

Wouldn't it be something if those shepherds—at least some of them—were still around when Jesus grew up and began announcing the kingdom of God? Because if they ever got the chance to hear Him speak, they would have realized that the *Savior* they saw that magical night outside Bethlehem offers rescue not just from the penalty of sin, but also from its power.

Jesus delivers eternally all who put their faith in Him. He'll also save us from a hundred other things daily, if only we'll ask Him. So, what is it that you need saving from . . .

Right *now*?

---

[*] The Bible doesn't say how many shepherds were "keeping watch over their flock by night."

6

IMAGE

A pattern, model, or visual representation of something else

The Son is the image of the invisible God, the firstborn over all creation.
(COLOSSIANS 1:15)

As the new grandparents blot their eyes, the first-time mom cuddles her sleeping newborn and smiles wearily. A pediatric nurse enters, glances at the infant, then back at the wide-eyed dad. "Mercy!" she exclaims with a shake of her head. "That baby is definitely his father's son!"

We can say it lots of ways: chip off the old block . . . spitting image . . . dead ringer . . . cut from the same cloth. Whichever expression we use, the idea is *strong resemblance*.

That's what the apostle Paul meant when he told some Christians in Colossae that Jesus (the Son) is "the *image* of the invisible God" (Colossians 1:15).

• • •

The Greek word translated "image" in our English Bibles is *eikon*. (This is where we get our English term *icon*.) Everyone has seen an icon. It's a portrait or symbol meant to remind us of or point to another person or thing.

According to the New Testament, Jesus of Nazareth was (and is) an icon—a living picture—of God Almighty. Hebrews 1:3 calls Him "the exact representation" of God's being.

These brain-straining pronouncements mean that if we want to know what God is like, we only need to look at Christ. Jesus said it himself, "Anyone who has seen me has seen the Father" (John 14:9). According to John 1:18, that's actually one of the primary reasons Jesus came—to *explain* the Almighty (NASB), to *reveal* Him (NLT), to *make the invisible God known* to the world (NIV).

● ● ●

A lot of people read the Old Testament and come away with an unsettling picture of God. Perhaps you've heard the complaints (perhaps you've made them yourself): Why is the God of Abraham so stern and aloof? Why is the God of Sinai so unpredictable and unapproachable?

This is why it's necessary to read the rest of the Bible—the New Testament. It's not that God changes; it's that He *reveals himself more fully in Christ.* In Jesus, God comes so close we can hear His heartbeat.

● ● ●

Realizing that God is like Jesus (because Jesus *is* God incarnate) can revolutionize a person's faith.

So can this related truth: We're icons too. *We* bear God's *image*—that's the word used in Genesis 1:27. This means humans have extraordinary capacities, creatively, intellectually, emotionally, morally, and relationally. It means we have enormous dignity and worth . . . and astonishing potential.

Think of all that might be possible if we'd only allow the living Christ to live in and through us!

7

MAGI

Wise men or astrologers from the East (likely Persia)
who sought the newborn Christ

After Jesus was born in Bethlehem in Judea, during the time of
King Herod, Magi from the east came to Jerusalem. (MATTHEW 2:1)

Each December we engage in the curious custom of singing
about three gift-bearing kings from the "Orient," being led
by a star of wonder and doing a lot of "traversing."

Or if we don't sing about them, we at least display figurines
of these guys. Most nativity sets feature a trio of regal-looking,
somber-faced, camel-riding strangers. The typical manger scene
groups these so-called wise men—together with a few shepherds—
around the baby Jesus (who usually looks more like a toddler than
a newborn, and who often appears to be waving).

Never mind the fact that the Gospels contain almost none
of these "facts."

Matthew doesn't number these mysterious visitors (much less
name them).* He never suggests they were royalty. He simply calls
them "Magi."

• • •

What's a *Magi*? Actually, the word is the plural form of *Magus*. The
Jewish historian Herodotus wrote about an order of Persian

---

* Tradition gives the names of the Magi as Balthasar, Gaspar, and Melchior.

priests (perhaps practitioners of Zoroastrianism) who said wise things, interpreted dreams, offered sacrifices, and studied astrology. In other words, think of a Magus as a fortune-teller with a PhD—somebody ancient kings kept on speed dial.

Question: So why would a bunch of pagan Magi go tromping across the desert to see Christ? Answer: Scholars argue (compellingly) that the witness and legacy of the Jews who had been exiled to Babylon back in the sixth century BC prompted the Magi's diligent search for the "king of the Jews" (Matthew 2:2). It's possible that leading up to the time of Christ, the Magi had access to the Old Testament writings belonging to those Jews who elected to remain in Persia (even after King Cyrus told them they were free to return to Jerusalem in 539 BC).

● ● ●

Who the Magi were is less important than what the Magi did . . . dropping—and risking—*everything* to travel hundreds of miles to catch a glimpse of a king so great, even the stars were talking about Him (see Psalm 19).

Matthew indicates that by the time these wise men reached Bethlehem, the shepherds were long gone, and the child and His mother were in a "house" (Matthew 2:11). Upon arrival, the Magi were "overjoyed" (Matthew 2:10)—literally, "exceedingly, deliriously glad." They "bowed down" or, as some translations put it, "fell down" and worshipped. Then they "opened their treasures" (their containers for valuables) and "presented one another with gifts."

No! (Just checking to see if you're still tracking.) They "presented *him* with gifts of gold, frankincense and myrrh" (Matthew 2:11; emphasis added).*

---

* The fact that the Magi gave Jesus three gifts is surely the reason most people assume there were three wise men. (Clearly, these people have never worked in an office where ten people can—and often do—pitch in to buy a single present.)

• • •

The lessons we could glean from the wise men are too many to list here, but how about this basic one: God is *always* speaking— through ancient holy writings, through nature, through the lives of the faithful—and *always* calling all sorts of fascinating people to himself.

Maybe we should perk up and pay closer attention?

8

MAN

The generic word for a human being

For there is one God and one mediator between God and mankind,
the man Christ Jesus. (1 TIMOTHY 2:5)

For two thousand years, people have been wrestling with the question, Who is Jesus?

In the first few centuries of the Christian movement, some groups (like the Arians and the Ebionites) decided that Christ wasn't divine—He was just a really remarkable person. Others (like the Docetists and Apollinarians) insisted Christ *was* divine, but not truly human (at least not in the same way we are). Still others (like the Nestorians) denied the union of His two natures in one person. Or (like the Eutychians), they put His human and divine natures into a kind of theological blender and mixed them together.

Meanwhile Orthodox Christianity has consistently taught that Jesus was (and is) fully God *and* fully man, one person with two distinct natures.

This God-man idea isn't *irrational* . . . it's *supra-rational*. It transcends human understanding. Holding the tension of such a mysterious doctrine stretches our minds to the breaking point. But hold it we must. Otherwise, we miss the truth about Jesus.

• • •

The Greek word translated "man" is *anthropos*, which, as you likely guessed, is the source of our English word *anthropology*. Biblically, this word is used to designate a human being (either male or female). In some contexts, it refers specifically to a male human. And—surprise!—this is the word the Bible uses in multiple places to speak of Jesus. He was a male, flesh and blood, living, breathing, walking, talking human being of Jewish descent (John 4:9). The New Testament writers called Him a man (Romans 5:15; 1 Corinthians 15:21). So did His enemies (John 10:33; 19:5).

●　●　●

The incarnate Son of God didn't just dip His toe into the human experience. He dived in headfirst. Practically, this means He was an infant who soiled himself. A kid who burped loudly (and likely belly laughed). A teen who survived the awkwardness of puberty. A young adult who battled an occasional stomach bug and smashed His thumb with a hammer and had bad morning breath.

Some say such talk is irreverent, that it demeans the Lord. I say it makes the Lord more amazing and intriguing. As a true human, He understands everything we're up against. And, as Paul explained to Timothy, His authentic humanity qualifies Him to stand between us and God, and serve as mediator (1 Timothy 1:5; see also Hebrews 2:14; 1 John 4:1–3).

●　●　●

The question of Christ's nature isn't an either-or question (divine *or* human?). It's a both-and proposition (divine *and* human). The old preacher Charles Spurgeon said it well: "He was a real Man. . . . Believe in Jesus as Man. You would be indignant at anyone who would diminish the Glory of His Godhead and most justly so, but oh, do not, yourself take away from Him the truth of His Humanity."

9

CARPENTER

*A craftsman who works primarily with wood
(or stone or metal)*

"Isn't this the carpenter? Isn't this Mary's son and the brother of James,
Joseph, Judas and Simon? Aren't his sisters here with us?" And they took
offense at him. (MARK 6:3)

In describing Jesus, the eternal Son of God, the apostle Paul
wrote, "By Him all things were created" (Colossians 1:16 NASB).
This means Jesus is the maker of electrons and elephants . . .
waterfalls and watermelons . . . black holes and black widow spiders.
All things.

Should we be surprised, then, that when the second member
of the holy Trinity came into the very world He'd built, He spent
most of His life here as a carpenter? Imagine that: The Maker
of the universe crafting things in some nondescript shop in Nazareth, Israel.

● ● ●

In Matthew 13:55, Jesus is described as "the carpenter's son."
In Mark 6:3, He's called "the carpenter."

These are the only two times the word *tekton* is used in the
New Testament. In extrabiblical Greek, it can, depending on the

context, mean builder, woodworker, or craftsman who works with stone or metal. In Hebrews 11:10, a related word—*technites*—is translated "architect."

The obvious implication is that Jesus, like most Jewish boys, went into the family business. Presumably He apprenticed under His father Joseph. Then from the time of His bar mitzvah (at age thirteen) until the time He changed careers (to engage in full-time ministry as an itinerant rabbi) at about age thirty (Luke 3:23) Jesus made things. He was a designer-builder. Justin Martyr, who lived from AD 100–165, said that Jesus built ploughs and yokes. God only knows if that's accurate, and if so, what else might He have built? Wagons? Tables? Chairs?

• • •

It's stunning to realize that for the longest portion of His life, Jesus *wasn't* preaching or healing or doing any of the things people associate with "saving the world." Rather, He was doing a lot of measuring (twice) and cutting (once). He spent more than half His life hammering and sanding. As best we can tell, His human experience involved way more sawdust than sermons.

And don't forget that the Gospels quote God the Father as saying He was "well pleased" with His Son . . . *before* Jesus ever began public ministry (Matthew 3:17; Mark 1:11; Luke 3:22). Clearly, pounding nails can be just as God-honoring a work as preaching to souls.

• • •

The fact that Jesus pleased God as a *carpenter* means you can make God smile in your calling. Are you a teacher? Then teach with excellence. Use your skills and platform for the kingdom of God. Are you a small business owner? Run your business the way Jesus would run it if He were sitting at your desk. Whatever you do, do it for God's glory (1 Corinthians 10:31). In short, use your training and experience—your job—to join the Carpenter in the greatest building project of all—the building of His church (Matthew 16:18).

10

APPEARANCE

The look of something or someone

He grew up before him like a tender shoot, and like a root out of dry ground. He had no beauty or majesty to attract us to him, nothing in his appearance that we should desire him. (ISAIAH 53:2)

The Bible describes the looks of multiple Bible characters:

- "Joseph was well-built and handsome" (Genesis 39:6).
- Eglon, the king of Moab, wasn't just carrying a few extra pounds from the holidays; he was "very fat" (Judges 3:17).*
- King Saul was "as handsome a young man as could be found anywhere in Israel, and he was a head taller than anyone else" (1 Samuel 9:2).
- David "was ruddy, with beautiful eyes and a handsome appearance" (1 Samuel 16:12 NASB).
- Goliath was somewhere around 9'9" tall (1 Samuel 17:4).
- Abigail was a "beautiful woman" (1 Samuel 25:3).

Yet when it comes to the physical appearance of the Bible's central character, we're left scratching our heads.

---

* If you're a *Star Wars* fan, think Jabba the Hutt.

• • •

The prophet Isaiah gave future generations of Jews some odd tips on how to recognize the coming Messiah. "Here's what He *won't* look like," Isaiah essentially said. "He'll have no beauty or majesty . . . nothing in his appearance to make people desire him."

The word *appearance* refers, of course, to that which is seen with the eye, the external look of a person or thing. It's what we notice right away: the perfect hair, flawless complexion, and million-dollar smile—or the crooked teeth, dirty face, and raggedy clothes.

Our eyes are drawn to "beautiful people"—the ones who ooze wealth, power, privilege. They're the kind of people whom people-watchers love to watch. The paparazzi hover like buzzards.

Isaiah's point seems to be that the Messiah would not be a heartthrob in the mold of George Clooney or King Saul. "If you see Him on the street and don't already know who He is, you won't give Him a second thought. Nothing about His appearance is going to make you look twice."

• • •

It's fascinating to see how artists and filmmakers have portrayed Jesus over the centuries. In fact, see for yourself. Google "images of Jesus." In most of the pictures, He looks less like a carpenter from the Middle East and more like a theater major from the Midwest. Decidedly waspish, fair (often pallid) complexion, piercing blue eyes, hair about shoulder-length. Sometimes He looks androgynous. Always He has a beard (maybe because in another passage from the pen of Isaiah, there's a mention of the future Messiah's enemies plucking out His beard [Isaiah 50:6]).

• • •

For people living in a culture that increasingly values appearance over substance, the fact that the Bible says almost nothing about Christ's appearance is refreshing. It meshes perfectly with at least three other big themes that permeate Scripture: Things are seldom what they seem. Heaven's values are a far cry from earth's. God looks at the heart.

DEVIL

A spiritual creature—many believe the highest of the
fallen angels—who opposes God, His people, and His plan

Then Jesus was led by the Spirit into the wilderness to be tempted by the devil.

(MATTHEW 4:1)

We can't adequately examine the life of Jesus without focusing, at least briefly, on the *devil*.

I know, I know . . . In many circles, bringing up the figure the Bible calls Satan, the evil one, Beelzebul, and the father of lies (among other names) causes heads to shake and eyes to roll. We may as well say we believe the earth is flat . . . or that Ironman is a real person and a true story.

We'd ignore this word—except for the fact that the gospel writers show Jesus talking matter-of-factly *about* (and even *to*) an actual being called the *devil*.

• • •

Our English word *diabolical* comes from the Greek word translated *devil* in the New Testament. That should tell us all we need to know. *Diabolos* means accuser or slanderer, which is precisely what we see the devil doing all the way through Scripture.

- When the serpent tempted Adam and Eve in Genesis 3, he did so by subtly suggesting that God was withholding Eden's best gift from them.
- When the devil tempted Jesus in the wilderness, he did so by slyly implying that God's plans for Jesus were needlessly difficult and downright dumb.
- When the apostle John got his famous glimpse of future things, he saw the devil vividly, and described him as "the accuser of our brothers and sisters" (Revelation 12:10).

● ● ●

Think about this: Where did the early church get the details about Christ's temptation by the devil (Matthew 4:1–11; Mark 1:12–13; Luke 4:1–13)? Clearly this information could only have come from Jesus himself—there were no other witnesses! Christ must have talked about this incident with His disciples. In numerous other places, Jesus is shown speaking openly and regularly about the devil (Matthew 12:26; Luke 8:12; 10:18; 13:16–18; 22:31; John 8:44).

His followers saw enough that they were convinced. Why else would Peter warn, "Be alert and of sober mind. Your enemy the devil prowls around like a roaring lion looking for someone to devour. Resist him" (1 Peter 5:8–9)? Or why would James plead, "Submit yourselves, then, to God. Resist the devil, and he will flee from you" (James 4:7)?

● ● ●

The teaching of the New Testament is that the devil is not only real, but extremely powerful, active, and dangerous. In truth, he'd very much like to have us for lunch.

But don't freak out. Instead, cling to the words of the apostle John, "The reason the Son of God appeared was to destroy the devil's work" (1 John 3:8). And take your stand on the promise of Paul, "The God of peace will soon crush Satan under your feet" (Romans 16:20).

IT IS WRITTEN

A one-word phrase used by Jesus to refer to the
truth and will of God, set down in words that men
might read, believe, and live

Jesus answered, "It is written: 'Man shall not live on bread alone, but on
every word that comes from the mouth of God.'" (Matthew 4:4)

All day every day, we face decisions. As we do we mull over
questions like these:

- What do I *feel* like doing?
- What's my *gut* telling me?
- What would my *friends* recommend?
- What are *other people* doing?
- What does *common sense* dictate?
- What do the *experts* say?
- What would benefit me most right now, or later,
  or perhaps now *and* later?
- What's the most convenient/fun/challenging/attention-
  getting (take your pick) option here?

Jesus, when confronted with some huge decisions early
in His ministry, asked and answered a different question: What
does *God* say?

• • •

Most people know the story. Repeatedly tempted by the devil (see chapter 11) to deviate from God's plan at the outset of His ministry, Jesus responded by saying, "It is written . . . it is written . . . it is written." (We also find this phrase on His lips other places in the Gospels.)

It's a three-word phrase in English but a single word in the Greek New Testament.* Here it means God's eternal truth, His revealed will, inscribed (on stone, parchment, or papyrus) so that humanity might read it, know it, and be transformed by it.

Think about that. Rather than letting fleshly desires, popular opinion, or the sly suggestions of the evil one guide Him, Jesus said, in so many words, "No thanks. I'll base my choices on what God has said (on what His servants and prophets have written down)."

• • •

Apart from the biblical writings, we'd know very little about God's character or will. Without holy Scripture we wouldn't know the good news of Christ's life, death, resurrection, and eventual return. The written Word of God is an incomparable gift to the world.

In his *Confessions,* Augustine tells of sitting one day under a fig tree and hearing a still, small voice. "Take it and read, take it and read." He recognized this as God urging him to pick up the Bible. He obeyed, and his life was forever changed. Likewise, John Wesley said that the turning point of his life came when he began praying to become a man of one book.

• • •

---

* The perfect passive indicative, third person singular form of the Greek word *grapho.*

Today as you face assorted choices, you'll likely swirl with questions (and hear a myriad of competing voices). How can you obey God's truth if you don't know it? This means a deep dive into Scripture. The right response to "It is written"?

"I am reading . . . and obeying."

13

LAMB

A young sheep; a common sacrificial animal in the Bible

The next day John saw Jesus coming toward him and said, "Look, the Lamb of God, who takes away the sin of the world!" (JOHN 1:29)

Unless you're into wool farming (or you work at a petting zoo), you probably don't come across very many lambs during the average work week.

In the Old Testament, however, lambs were everywhere. And in the New Testament, John the Baptist burst on the scene and started introducing Jesus to everyone within earshot as "the Lamb of God" (John 1:29, 36). The apostle Peter employed this same terminology in his first epistle (1 Peter 1:19). The apostle John—in Revelation, that cryptic book of visions—used the word *lamb* frequently to refer to Jesus.

What was lamb-like about Jesus? Why is this term important?

• • •

Anyone beyond the age of three knows that a *lamb* is a young sheep. In ancient Jewish culture lambs were valued for their meat, wool, and skin (used to make fine parchment known as vellum). Lambs were also a key part of Jewish worship. Burnt offerings, peace offerings, sin offerings—all these sacrifices called for innocent and spotless (nondefective) lambs. Lambs also featured prominently in the annual Passover celebration and other Jewish festivals.

Two different Greek words are translated *lamb* in the New Testament. One of them is found only four times, and always refers in a figurative way to Jesus Christ. This is the word John the Baptist used.

● ● ●

When John called Jesus "the Lamb of God, who takes away the sin of the world," he was thinking ahead to Christ's death and thinking back on the original Passover observance in Egypt, just before the Exodus. Reread Exodus 12, and you'll see that the Jews were saved from judgment when they applied the blood of a "Passover" lamb to the doorframes of their homes.

It could be that John was also thinking of Isaiah 53. In that famous passage, Isaiah foresaw the day when a coming Messiah would be "led like a lamb to the slaughter" (v. 7). This Servant of the Lord would suffer and make "his life an offering for sin" (v. 10) and by that sacrificial act, bear "the sin of many" (v. 12).

In Revelation this same imagery is used. Christ is described several times there as a Lamb that once *was* slain (5:6–9, 12; 13:8)—but is no longer.

● ● ●

To most people, the idea of animal sacrifice seems primitive at best and barbaric at worst. And the idea that God put His own Son Jesus to death so that He wouldn't have to punish sinners makes a lot of folks skittish around the Almighty.

Here's what we need to remember: Jesus understood and accepted His role as the Lamb of God. In fact, the night before His crucifixion, with the remnants of a Passover meal on the table in front of them, Jesus gave bread and wine to His followers and essentially told them, "From now on, celebrate the truth of my body broken for you and my blood 'poured out . . . for the forgiveness of sins'" (Matthew 26:28).

Bottom line, if the ultimate sacrificial Lamb was okay with the concept of a sacrificial lamb, shouldn't we be?

MESSIAH

One anointed by God to deliver and rule over
God's chosen people

Mary was the mother of Jesus who is called the Messiah.

(MATTHEW 1:16)

Each presidential election cycle we long for a larger-than-life statesman like George Washington or John Adams (obviously forgetting that if smartphones and social media had been around in the late 1700s, we might not think so highly of our Founding Fathers today).

We pine for a wise, pragmatic leader like Abraham Lincoln, a great communicator like Ronald Reagan, a strong commander-in-chief like Dwight D. Eisenhower, or a comforting father figure like FDR. Still others look for a brash, outspoken candidate like Teddy Roosevelt (to shake up the status quo) . . . My point being that the word *president* means very different things to different people.

Among the Jews, the comparably "loaded" word was (and still is) *Messiah.*

● ● ●

Messiah is a Hebrew title that means "anointed one" (it's translated "Christ" from the Greek *Christos*). In Old Testament times, Jewish priests and kings weren't sworn in while raising their right hand (as US presidents and judges are); they were anointed with oil. This ceremony symbolically set them apart for the task before them. As "anointed ones," these leaders were, in the most literal sense, *messiahs.*

However, numerous Old Testament Scriptures refer—sometimes cryptically, other times with great specificity—to one individual who would be the *ultimate* anointed of God. This Messiah (capital M) would be the Leader above all leaders. He'd come from the tribe of Judah (Genesis 49:10), be a descendant of King David (2 Samuel 7:16), a priest like Melchizedek (Psalm 110:4), a prophet like the deliverer Moses (Deuteronomy 18:15–19), and the Lord's choice servant (Isaiah 42:1–4). In short, this One would usher in an unparalleled era of peace and justice and prosperity (Isaiah 9:6–7).

In one ancient passage, the coming Messiah actually explained His (then future) ministry: "to proclaim good news to the poor . . . to bind up the brokenhearted, to proclaim freedom for the captives and release from darkness for the prisoners, to proclaim the year of the LORD's favor and the day of vengeance of our God" (Isaiah 61:1–2).

● ● ●

With so many prophecies focusing on different qualities of God's Anointed One, it's not hard to see why the Jewish people had differing expectations about Messiah. Generally speaking, however, by the time of Jesus, most believed that Messiah would be a deliverer-king who would liberate Israel from Roman oppression. And perhaps like Moses and the other prophets, He'd work some miracles too.

As far as the prophecy of a coming Servant of God who would suffer greatly (Isaiah 52–53) . . . nobody really seemed to understand that passage as pertaining to Messiah.

• • •

An angel, informing the shepherds about the child born in Bethle-hem, introduced Him as "the Messiah" (Luke 2:11). Three decades later, when Jesus began His public ministry, He read Isaiah 61 (cited above)* to a synagogue full of people and calmly said, "Today this scripture is fulfilled in your hearing" (Luke 4:21).

You may not accept Jesus as the promised Messiah, but there's no denying that's what He—and the New Testament—claims He is.

---

* Stopping before the last phrase about "the day of vengeance of our God."

15

PROPHET

One called by God to be a divine spokesperson
or mouthpiece

After the people saw the sign Jesus performed, they began to say, "Surely
this is the Prophet who is to come into the world." (JOHN 6:14)

I f you conducted a one-question survey, Who is Jesus?, you'd
get a wide array of answers: Fictional character. Savior.
Misunderstood Jewish rabbi. Revolutionary who got squashed
by the Romans. Self-proclaimed Messiah. Son of God. Great
moral teacher (on a par with Buddha or Confucius).

Many would likely reply, "He was a prophet."

Is that true? Was Jesus a prophet?

• • •

In his final remarks to the nation of Israel, old Moses spoke of a coming day when "the LORD your God will raise up for you a prophet
like me from among you.... You must listen to him" (Deuteronomy
18:15). Most scholars agree this is one of the Bible's earliest predictions of a coming *Messiah* (see previous chapter). Throughout their
history—and especially during oppressive times—the Israelites
clung to Moses's cryptic words. Every time a powerful leader
showed up, the buzz would begin, and people would wonder, *Is this
the Prophet that Moses spoke about?* (see John 1:21).

This kind of speculation reached a fever pitch when Jesus took the equivalent of a little boy's Happy Meal and fed thousands in the wilderness (John 6:1–13). The miracle was shades of "the good old days," when God and Moses provided the Israelites with manna (bread from heaven).

• • •

Prophets have a straightforward job description: announce God's truth to the world. They do this in two basic ways: *foretelling* and *forthtelling*. *Foretelling* ("declaring things before they happen") is what most people think of when they think about *prophets*. However, *forthtelling* is equally important. This is declaring the truth of God in a forthright manner. Through forthtelling, prophets challenge listeners to align their hearts and lives with God's will right *now*.

The New Testament says Jesus *was* the prophet Moses had talked about. It shows Him engaging in plenty of forthtelling. And in the foretelling department, He correctly prophesied, among other things, the building of His church (Matthew 16:17–18), the destruction of Jerusalem and the temple (Luke 21:5–6), Judas's betrayal (Matthew 26:20–25), Peter's denial (Matthew 26:34), His own death (Matthew 16:21; Mark 8:31), and the coming of the Holy Spirit (John 16:7–15). He also spoke matter-of-factly about returning to earth at some point in the future (Matthew 24:42; Luke 21:27).

• • •

Jesus was a lot *more* than a prophet, but He was a prophet. At the least, then, you and I need to wrestle with His astonishing claim: "I say only what I have heard from the one who sent me, and he is completely truthful" (John 8:26 NLT). And we need to grapple with His pointed question: "If I am telling the truth, why don't you believe me?" (John 8:46).

PREACH

To announce or declare news

After Jesus had finished instructing his twelve disciples, he went on from there to teach and preach in the towns of Galilee. (MATTHEW 11:1)

Ask five people to explain the difference between teaching and preaching. Bet you a cup of dark roast coffee you'll hear responses like these:

- Preachers get animated and yell a lot; teachers are more analytical and inclined to drone on and on.
- Preaching is meant to be inspirational—it's aimed at the heart. Teaching, on the other hand, is informational—it's aimed at the head.
- Preaching is supposed to have a "main point" or "big idea"; teaching is supposed to cover all the details.

Are any of these distinctions correct? *Is* there a difference between teaching and preaching?

• • •

Matthew, one of Christ's most devoted followers, tells us that Jesus engaged in both *teaching and preaching*. (Note: With that statement, the author of the first gospel indicated there *is* a difference between those two activities.)

The word translated *teach* means to provide or impart instruction, to engage in discourse and explain a thing. The word translated *preach* means to declare or to proclaim big, breaking news. In ancient times, a king would dispatch heralds hither and yon throughout his kingdom to preach—to spread the word about important events. They'd enter village after village crying, "The king is coming!" or "Our enemies just surrendered!" or "A royal heir has been born!"—that sort of thing. Preaching, in the most literal, biblical sense, is nothing more than announcing or publicizing significant news.

●　●　●

Mark's gospel begins with Jesus "proclaiming [preaching] the good news of God." His short announcement? "The kingdom of God has come near. Repent and believe the good news" (Mark 1:14–15). A few verses later, Mark records Jesus saying, "Let us go somewhere else—to the nearby villages—so I can preach there also. That is why I have come" (Mark 1:38).

We often think that preaching means a pulpit, a big floppy Bible, a large audience, and a sweaty, worked-up preacher (who talks loudly and gestures wildly). In truth, when we tell a depressed coworker, "There is a God who loves you—and His name is Jesus Christ," we are engaging in the best kind of gospel preaching.

●　●　●

Because preaching—in the New Testament sense—is simply declaring facts about Jesus, it never has to devolve into arguments, defensiveness, or angry words. Our goal isn't to change minds (only the Spirit of God can do that). We simply announce. We broadcast the good news.

When we do this we sometimes get asked a *lot* of questions. This gives us the chance to do a little teaching to provide extra explanation and clarification.

Want to be like Jesus today? Ask God for the chance to do a little preaching and teaching.

17

GOSPEL

An announcement of good news (in the Bible the
ultimate Good News that Jesus lived sinlessly,
died sacrificially, and rose triumphantly . . . all in order
to save those who would put their trust in Him)

The beginning of the gospel of Jesus Christ, the Son of God.

(MARK 1:1 NASB)

If there's one practice at which we humans excel, it's announcing good news. We don't have to be prompted to share stories like, "I found this $5 painting at a garage sale . . . and then learned it's an original Monet." We broadcast good news automatically, instinctively, effortlessly. We're naturals.

Don't believe it? Go check your various social media feeds and note the sorts of things people are posting. Guaranteed it'll be full of announcements like these:

- I set my PR in the half marathon!
- We're engaged!
- Finally boarding the plane! Hawaii bound!
- I'm a granddad!
- They accepted our offer!
- My daughter passed the bar! (the exam, not the tavern—although many would see their kid passing a tavern as good news too)

We can't keep quiet about good news . . . which brings up the issue of the *gospel* of Jesus.

• • •

Gospel literally means "glad tidings" or "good news." In the Old Testament, people routinely broadcast all sorts of good news: births (Jeremiah 20:15); military victories over enemies (1 Samuel 31:9); the choice of a new king (1 Kings 1:42); personal deliverance from trouble (Psalm 40:9); and, of course, the remarkable blessing of God's salvation (Psalm 96:2).

In the New Testament, Jesus is the personification of God's Good News. His coming reveals heaven's intention to rescue sinners and restore all things. In His first advent, Jesus inaugurated the righteous rule of God. His perfect life, sacrificial death, and glorious resurrection provided a way for sinners to be reconciled to God; it also opened the door for the immeasurable blessings promised in the Old Testament. At His second coming, Jesus will reign forever over a world that's received the ultimate makeover.

• • •

Did you know we get our English word *evangelism* from the New Testament Greek word that's translated *gospel*? This means people who embrace Jesus and His teachings are, in a strict sense, *evangelicals*, people of the gladdest tidings. They are to be *evangelists*. They are to engage in *evangelism*.

And yet many don't. Which prompts the question, If the message of Jesus is such good news, why the reluctance to talk about it? (This might be a good question to bat around with your Christian friends.)

• • •

If the message of Jesus has lost its pizzazz in your heart, take an hour or two to reread the gospel of Mark in one sitting. Before you start, pray what David prayed, "Restore to me the joy of your salvation" (Psalm 51:12).

REPENT

A change in one's thinking that leads to a
change in one's direction

From that time on Jesus began to preach, "Repent, for the kingdom of
heaven has come near." (MATTHEW 4:17)

Repent!
This is the Bible word some believers like to spray-paint on highway overpasses.* Attend a revival meeting (especially in the Deep South), and there's a 100 percent guarantee the worked-up preacher will find a way to work the word into his message . . . several times.

The word makes most people flinch and wince, cringe and duck. The way it sometimes gets hurled around, it can feel like the equivalent of a spiritual flogging.

But what if that's a gross misunderstanding of the word? What if, instead of an angry condemnation, *repent* is actually a gracious invitation?

• • •

According to Matthew, Jesus began His public ministry by announcing the arrival of the kingdom of heaven and urging people to repent. (Mark added ". . . and believe the good news!")

---

* My friend Dave calls this practice "evandelism."

In the Hebrew Scriptures, the word often translated "repent" means "to turn around, return, come back." In the New Testament, the word literally means "to change your mind." Put those two ideas together and *repent* means "to get new information and, as a result, go in a new direction." Or we might say it's getting a truer view of reality and, as a result, doing a one-eighty.

That driver who complied with the flashing sign, "Bridge out ahead. Make a U-turn now," is, in the most literal sense, repentant. The other driver, the one who ignored the warning and barreled ahead is . . . ahem . . . no longer with us.

● ● ●

Notice that Jesus was calling on people to *repent* in the context of announcing *good news* (for example, the kingdom of heaven being near, because the king of heaven was present!). Question: Who announces good news with a scowl and in a scolding voice? Answer: Nobody. Jesus wasn't angry when He cried, "Repent!" If anything, He was pleading, "I'm here at last! You don't have to keep chasing after things that can never satisfy your empty soul. Stop. Turn around and come to me. Let me give you new life, eternal life, life to the fullest extent."

What about *that* message would make anyone wince or duck?

● ● ●

The prerequisite for repentance is humility. You can't be stubborn. You can't buy into the crazy idea that you are always right. You will never be open to what's true as long as you are clinging tightly to what's false. You can't move in the right direction as long as you insist on going the wrong way.

Let Jesus help you repent. He's not only willing, He's gentle. If you ask Him for insight, He'll show where wrong thoughts have led to wrong acts (and sometimes to bad habits that are taking you far from where you want to be).

And for the record, His command to "repent and believe the good news!" (Mark 1:15) isn't just how we begin the Christian life; it's how we're called to live every day until He calls us home.

19

BELIEVE

To put trust in; to accept as reliable, or embrace as true

Jesus answered, "The work of God is this: to believe in the one he has sent."
(JOHN 6:29)

Jews in the first century wrestled with the same big question people in the twenty-first century wonder about. We phrase it in a variety of ways. "How can I know I'm right with my Maker?" Or "If there's a heaven, how can I be sure I'll go there when I die?" Or "What do I have to do in order to have eternal life?"

Jesus's answer was short, sweet, and shocking. "Here's what you have to do: Believe. Believe in the one [God] has sent." In other words, "Put your trust in *me*."

Can it really be that simple? And if so, what does that even mean? What does it mean to *believe*?

• • •

The Old Testament word translated *believe** means to regard something—a statement, a promise, someone's message—as reliable and to accept that thing as true (1 Kings 10:7; Psalm 106:12).

---

* The Hebrew word is *'aman*. Elsewhere it's used in reference to a pillar that proves to be firm and reliable.

It can also mean to deem a person trustworthy—and therefore to put your trust in that one (Genesis 15:6). It's the same in the New Testament. The word *believe** simply means to have faith in someone or something.

The apostle John, author of the fourth gospel, had much to say about this topic.[†] On at least two occasions he implied there's such a thing as inadequate or defective faith (John 2:23–25; 8:30–59). In the first instance, it's clear that Jesus wasn't buying some people's "belief." In the second, Jesus ended up calling some "believers" children of the devil! They, in turn, accused Him of being demon-possessed!

• • •

Perhaps something John wrote at the beginning of his gospel clears up the mystery of what true, saving belief is. Noting that many Jewish people did not "receive" Jesus (literally, they did not accept His teaching and "take him to themselves"), John then wrote, "Yet to all who did receive him, to those who believed in his name, he gave the right to become children of God" (John 1:12). Here, John seems to equate believing in Jesus with receiving Jesus. In other words, belief in Jesus is more than nodding one's head at a list of religious ideas; it's welcoming and embracing a living person.

• • •

It's true that we can't please God without faith (Hebrews 11:6). It's also true that not every kind of belief pleases God. James, the half brother of Jesus, warned about "dead faith" (James 2:17)

---

* The Greek word is *pisteuo*, and it means "to put faith in, to trust in, or to entrust one's self to."
† Of the approximate 250 occurrences of the verb *pisteuo* in the New Testament, 98 are found in the fourth gospel! (Matthew, Mark, and Luke only use the word 36 times total.) No wonder John is sometimes called "the gospel of belief."

and noted a couple verses later (v. 19) that even demons believe orthodox theology about God.

Here's the bottom line: Have you put your trust in Jesus the person? Do you accept that He is who He claims to be? And do you accept, not just claims about Him, but Him?

If you're struggling with all this trust stuff, ask Jesus for help. After all, He's the one who said, "Apart from me you can do nothing" (John 15:5).

Fact is, we can't even believe properly without His assistance.

20

COME

To move toward, draw near, or arrive

"Come, follow me," Jesus said, "and I will send you out to fish for people."
(Matthew 4:19)

A t work you could decide to *come* out of your shell, *come* on like gangbusters, *come* up through the ranks—and perhaps see your professional dreams *come* true.

At home it's possible to *come* within a whisker of coming unglued . . . *come* to a screeching halt . . . *come* to your senses . . . and *come* back from the brink.

You can *come* to the aid of a friend today. *Come* full circle. *Come* to a conclusion. Refuse to cross any bridges before you *come* to them.

Just be sure that in all your coming (and going), you don't miss Jesus saying, "Come, follow me."

• • •

The word *come* suggests movement. It tantalizes us with the possibility of change. You are in one place, but you have the opportunity to leave that place and go someplace better. In the mouth of Christ, the word is a holy summons, a call to walk away from an old, dead-end life and to embark on a new life full of surprises and adventure.

In essence, Jesus says to those who trust Him, "Come along with me, follow where I lead, watch what I do, listen to what I say. Learn from me. As you come with me, you will be-come like me. I will transform you." That's what a disciple is and does. (Remember what Jesus said in Luke 6:40? A "student . . . who is fully trained will be like their teacher.")

• • •

Christ's command "Come" is an invitation to change. It's a call to become like Him. That's God's purpose for us. A basic rule of life is that we become like those we spend time with. You've seen this. Close friends pick up each other's expressions and manner-isms. Married couples often begin to think alike—and finish each other's sentences.

We are called by Christ, to Christ. And why? So that we might be with Him, become like Him, and learn to live for Him.

• • •

Before Christ ever tells anyone to go do anything, He first says come. "Come to me . . . for rest, healing, forgiveness, hope, cleansing, restoration." He calls to us most clearly through His written Word. He also summons us through the events of our lives, and by a hundred other means. What does He want? Your money? Your stuff? Your religious activity? No. He wants your heart. He wants you.

The only question is, Will we answer His decisive call to come and be His followers? According to Jesus this is more than having warm thoughts about Him. It's more than squeezing Him into whatever free time we have left after we've done everything else we want to do . . .

To come to Christ, we have to turn our backs on other things. Logically, going to Him means leaving some other things behind. And it's not a one-time decision. As one man put it, "It's one big 'YES!' followed by a lot of little 'okay's."

21

CALLED

To be summoned into relationship or commissioned
to do a certain task

Jesus called them, and immediately they left the boat and their father
and followed him. (MATTHEW 4:21–22)

It's one of the strangest scenes in all of Scripture: The carpenter-turned-rabbi who has everyone in Galilee buzzing stops to talk with Peter, Andrew, James, and John. Jesus calls *them* to abandon their careers as commercial fishermen and become His apprentices.

Stunning when you consider who and what these guys are. Not the sort of students who get voted Most Likely to Succeed at Hebrew school in Bethsaida. No, these are average Joes. Not super educated. Not from prominent families. Not—we discover reading the Gospels—exactly poster children for faith or love.

The whole scene is bizarre . . . and wildly encouraging at once. Think about it. The one calling this "nothing special" bunch to himself is making messianic claims, hinting (not so subtly) that He's divine. If true, He knows these recruits through and through (all their shortcomings, all their dirty little secrets). Yet *still* He calls them. "Come *to* me . . . come *with* me!"

In other words, "I pick you."

• • •

Call is a hugely important word in the Bible. When God is the one doing the calling, it refers to being summoned into relationship (1 Corinthians 1:9) or called to carry out a task (Exodus 3:4; Romans 1:1). Think of it as being handpicked or chosen.

• • •

Let this sink in. *God* was calling them. God was calling *them.*

Let something else sink in. Nothing has changed. Though Christ has ascended bodily into heaven, and though He won't be showing up physically this afternoon at your house or next Tuesday at your office, He hasn't stopped being the living Word of God. He still speaks. He still calls folks, still issues the invitation, "Come with me. Let's go!"

How does this work when He's no longer on earth?

• • •

Our Lord calls to us in a variety of ways. He speaks in a general way through creation (Psalm 19:1–6), a reality that prompted George Washington Carver to refer to nature as God's "unlimited broadcasting system." The Lord speaks in more specific ways through His written Word (Psalm 19:7–11).

God calls via other creative means too—through nudges by the Holy Spirit; through the encouragement of people (elders and preachers and writers and small group leaders and friends) who are following Christ; through sermons and songs; and through random events, circumstances, and trials. Malcolm Muggeridge once said, "All happenings great and small are parables whereby God speaks. The art of life is to get the message."

Here's what Jesus said, "My sheep listen to my voice; I know them, and they follow me" (John 10:27). The implication? We can't very well follow Jesus until we first hear His call.

22

FOLLOW

To accompany one who precedes;
to be an attendant or disciple of another

As Jesus went on from there, he saw a man named Matthew sitting at
the tax collector's booth. "Follow me," he told him, and Matthew got up
and followed him. (MATTHEW 9:9)

In the information age, *following* has been reduced to scrolling
and clicking.

If you've got a smartphone and internet access, you can follow almost anyone or anything: a coworker's European vacation, your child's daily progress at school, or—thanks to a live nest cam— the hatching and growth of baby bald eagles in Decorah, Iowa.

With the World Wide Web, you can follow along with the highs and lows of your favorite sports team, the ever-changing value of your 401(k), your friends' efforts to adopt a child from China, the campaign of a politician, the crazy life of a celebrity . . . blah, blah, blah.

What's more, when you get tired of any of those things or people, you can "unfollow" them with a simple click.

• • •

When Jesus told people, "Follow me," He meant something very different from "Add me to your Twitter feed" or "Sign up for my weekly blog post."

On the lips of Christ, the word *follow* had (and still has) monumental implications. The idea is something like, "Stop what you're doing and come be my student, for life. Trust me enough to accompany me wherever I lead you. Watch me. Listen to me. Do what I tell you. Model your life after my life."

In short, following Jesus is synonymous with being His disciple.

● ● ●

In the first century you couldn't "follow" a respected teacher online. Distance education? Subscribing to a YouTube channel? Signing up for email newsletters? Being part of some social media "tribe"? Sorry. Not possible.

Following a teacher required being with them—literally. You tagged along, paid attention, asked and answered questions.

● ● ●

All this raises one very obvious question: How do we go about following a teacher who's no longer physically present on the earth?

First, we have His (written) Word to guide us (if only we'll open it, wrestle with its implications, and take it to heart). Second, we have His indwelling Spirit to nudge and empower and transform us (if only we'll let Him fill us). Third, we have His people to encourage us (if only we'll participate in healthy Christian community). Fourth, it's together with our brothers and sisters in the faith that we discover His mission, helping others understand what it means to follow Jesus (if only we'll get up off the couch).

23

DISCIPLES

One who learns from and emulates another; a student or follower or apprentice or protégé

Therefore go and make disciples of all nations, baptizing them in the name of the Father and of the Son and of the Holy Spirit. (MATTHEW 28:19)

What exactly was the mission of Jesus? In His own *words*, He came to . . .

- Preach (the gospel; see Mark 1:38)
- Fulfill the law (Matthew 5:17)
- Seek and save the lost (Luke 19:10)
- Call sinners to repentance (Luke 5:32)
- Do the will of the Father (John 6:38)
- Give people abundant life (John 10:10)
- Suffer and die (John 12:27)
- Be a servant and give His life as a ransom for sin (Mark 10:45)
- Testify to the truth (John 18:37)

By His *actions*, it's clear He had one additional goal—to make *disciples*.

• • •

The word *disciple* means student or learner. A disciple attaches to a respected leader in order to obtain knowledge, to absorb wisdom, to learn the ropes of a particular trade, or to master a certain subject. It may help to think of an *apprentice* or *trainee*.

In first-century Judaism, respected teachers (rabbis) attracted large crowds of followers (of varying commitment levels). In devoting themselves fully to a teacher, *disciples* were essentially saying, "We want to learn how to think, talk, and act like this person."

• • •

Discipleship isn't a religious idea, per se. We see this same sort of passing on of vital information and skills in every sector of life: the arts, education, sports, business, politics, medicine, technology, etcetera. A business leader mentors three college interns. A successful coach imparts her philosophy to her staff. An esteemed professor pours into his graduate assistants. A judge guides and influences two clerks.

To the twelve guys He handpicked, and to the others who traveled and ministered with Him, Jesus gave invaluable, life-on-life, hands-on training. Jesus spent three years rubbing shoulders with them, downloading the truth of God into their hearts, and modeling servant leadership.

• • •

When it was time for Jesus to return to heaven, He told His disciples to carry on the mission. In so many words, He said, "Just as I've done with you, turn around and do with others. Go everywhere and make disciples in every nation. All that you've learned from me, pass on to others." It wasn't enough for Christ to come and die—He needed disciples who would make disciples, who would make disciples, who would . . . you get the idea.

Guess what? For those of us who claim to be Christ's followers, *being* disciples who *make* disciples is our mission too.

24

WITH

A preposition that suggests presence and, ideally,
connotes intimacy and togetherness

He appointed twelve that they might be with him and that he might send
them out to preach. (MARK 3:14)

Raise your hand if you've ever had this experience: You're eating dinner with friends . . . or on vacation with your family . . . but you're not truly *with* them.

Yes, yes, I see that hand.

Welcome to the gotta-do-it-all era, where the allure of multitasking has most us engaging in five or six activities at any given moment (and doing most or all of those things poorly). We're the generation that has perfected the illusion of "being there" without really being there. We know how to appear to be present when we're actually absent.

Maybe this is why before Jeus called His followers to engage in *witness*, He wanted them to perfect the art of *with-ness*.

• • •

The simple preposition *with* conveys the increasingly difficult idea of *presence*, which is more than just *accompanying another*. (Think *physical proximity that results in intimacy*.)

Thus, when Jesus called the twelve to follow Him and be His disciples, He was saying at the most basic level, "I want to be *with you*, and I want you to be *with me*. I want a relationship."

For Jesus, such with-ness meant being fully engaged. Wherever He was, He was "all there." This explains how Jesus was able to notice things that no one else saw, why He picked up on little details others missed. Jesus was never *not* in the moment.

• • •

Inherent in the idea of *with* is the idea of intentional togetherness. For the original disciples, this kind of with-ness with Jesus meant literally following Him around. If He went to Bethany, they tagged along. Modern-day believers can't follow Christ in quite the same way. Now, a relationship with Christ is spiritual in nature. Therefore, it's different from our other relationships that involve all our physical senses. You can *see* your coworker walk through the door. You can *hug* a friend who's heartbroken. You can *hear* your neighbor snicker while she tells you a funny story.

Because He's no longer physically present on the earth, we can't know Jesus in such ways. Except by faith.

By faith, we *can* hear Him speak (most clearly through reading His words in Scripture). By faith we *can* talk to Him (via honest, heartfelt prayer). By faith, we *can* even see Him—because He actually *does* have a body here on earth: the church. *We* Christians are His body. Meaning, when we spend time *with* other believers in big and small groups, we get occasional holy glimpses of Christ.

• • •

Be careful not to get the cart before the horse. In "church world," it's easy to jump immediately to busyness and ministry. Jesus, meanwhile, seems to emphasize, before anything else, relationship and intimacy.

Before we get too obsessed with all the things we think Jesus wants us doing *for* Him, let's remember the other essential part of a disciple's job description: simply being *with* Him.

25

KINGDOM

The rule of a monarch over a specific realm or territory

"The time has come," he said. "The kingdom of God has come near. Repent and believe the good news!" (MARK 1:15)

In a political era dominated by democracies and republics, the word *kingdom* no longer means what it once meant. Today, when people use the word, they're almost surely referring to some make-believe realm they've visited in a book or seen on a screen— places like Panem, Oz, Gondor, Narnia, or Cron.

See for yourself. Play the word association game at school or work tomorrow and throw out the word *kingdom*. See how many mention dragons or elves, Wookies or centaurs. Listen for mentions of lowly peasants serving some wealthy king or queen in a faraway castle—maybe an emperor ruling over a distant galaxy.

This will come as a shock to exactly no one, but Jesus wasn't referring to any of these things when He talked incessantly about the *kingdom* of God.

• • •

In the literal sense, a kingdom is a governing structure whereby a monarch (king or queen) rules over a certain area. In ancient times the Jewish people saw their nation as "God's kingdom." Yahweh had chosen them, provided them with a land in which to live, and given them kings (like mighty David and magnificent Solomon) to rule justly over them.

But this kingdom went the way of all earthly kingdoms. To put it bluntly, it went to pot and went away. The Jewish people turned away from God, so God sent them into exile. Many Jews eventually returned to the "promised land," but it wasn't the same. For six *centuries* leading up to the time of Christ, a parade of foreign kingdoms dominated the Jews and occupied their land.

Naturally, when Jesus showed up saying, "The kingdom of God has come near," every heart stopped beating momentarily—then started racing wildly.

• • •

What exactly did Jesus mean when He talked about "the kingdom of God"? An actual, earthly kingdom, over which He (as Messiah) would rule? The arrival of an invisible but real spiritual reign in the hearts of His followers? The answer depends on what preacher or theologian you listen to.

Everyone, however, agrees with this: The kingdom Jesus described was unlike any kingdom that's every existed anywhere. (Phrases like topsy-turvy and counterintuitive come to mind.) In so many words, Jesus said, "Imagine a kingdom where the qualification for citizenship is being *unqualified* . . . a populace full of humility and love—instead of themselves. Try to picture a place where leaders serve others instead of using and manipulating them . . . and where no one is left out because everyone—young, old, wealthy, poor, Jew, non-Jew, smart, dumb, beautiful, homely—is important and matters to God. In my crazy, upside-down kingdom, giving beats getting . . . substance—not appearance—is what matters . . . and small, seemingly 'nothing' things win out over big, showy things."

• • •

I personally believe Jesus is going to physically return to earth one day to reign and rule. Maybe you think that's wacky. That's okay. My feelings aren't hurt. I bet we can agree on this: Today we should offer ourselves to Jesus. Maybe with a prayer like this: "Reign in me, King Jesus. Rule over me. May your kingdom come in my heart, and may your will be done on earth—in and through my life. Amen."

26

CROWDS

Large groups of people

Early the next morning Jesus went out to an isolated place.
The crowds searched everywhere for him, and when they finally found
him, they begged him not to leave them. (LUKE 4:42 NLT)

In the Gospels, Jesus enjoyed occasional moments of solitude (Matthew 14:13; Mark 1:35) and private meetings with people (John 3, 4). More often, it seems, He interacted with large, boisterous *crowds*.

Eager multitudes stalked Him on foot, sometimes even by boat. Ancient flash mobs showed up at synagogues. They lined streets, crowded around Him on beaches, followed Him up mountainsides. When they weren't walking alongside Him, trying to touch Him, they were analyzing His every move and hanging on His every word. They simply wouldn't leave Him alone.

What can we say? Jesus was trending when Twitter was something only birds did. The desperate and the devout, the sick and the cynical—they turned out in droves, day after day, in hopes of catching a glimpse or, better yet, witnessing a miracle.

In the Gospels, the Savior is like a living island, surrounded by a vast sea of souls.

• • •

The biblical word translated *crowd* means—hold on to your hat—"a large group of people."

Not exactly life-changing. Yet Christ's *attitude toward crowds* most definitely is.

In Matthew 14:14, when Jesus saw yet another large crowd awaiting Him on the beach, He became surly and irritated. No! Jesus plunged into the horde and began healing the hurting.

In John 6, in front of a growing throng of followers, Jesus decided to "work the crowd" and "play to the masses" to increase His popularity, right? Wrong! Jesus almost seemed to go out of His way to say hard things that would thin the crowd. He knew all the research social scientists are only now discovering. Crowds are fickle, and often irrational. They're easily manipulated. "Mob mentality" is a real phenomenon.

● ● ●

When we find a group of people who think just like we do, it's easy to assume we're in the right camp, that there's safety in numbers. What a silly notion! Just because the fast-food franchise by the interstate is packed with people every day at lunch doesn't mean its burgers are all that great (or great for you).

Jesus said this shocking thing about crowds: If the road you're traveling through life is always crowded, you're on the wrong road (Matthew 7:13–14).

● ● ●

When Jesus encountered crowds, He didn't just see a blur of faces. He saw individuals with unique needs. In Jericho, He noted the adoring masses . . . then zeroed in on a tax official named Zacchaeus—the loneliest, most despised, most desperate man in town (Luke 19:1–10).

Maybe you feel lost in the crowd? Or part of the wrong crowd?

If so, take comfort: while most public figures obsess over the size of crowds, Jesus cares primarily about the individuals in them.

27

COMPASSION

A feeling of pity or concern that sparks caring actions

When he saw the crowds, he had compassion on them, because they were harassed and helpless, like sheep without a shepherd. (MATTHEW 9:36)

Why was Matthew (more than the other gospel writers) so quick to note the *compassion* of Jesus? Probably because during his years as a tax collector, he'd mostly been met with scornful looks, heartless comments, and cold indifference.

When we're bowled over by something (for example, Paul by God's grace or John by Christ's love), it's human nature to talk about it incessantly.

• • •

This likely explains Matthew's references to the Lord's sadness for the troubled masses (14:14; 15:32), His sorrow for hurting individuals (20:34).

The Greek word translated "compassion" in the New Testament is related to the word for bowels or intestines. It's the idea of being moved deeply, torn up internally. We see folks in desperate trouble—storm survivors, starving kids, victims of yet another mass shooting—and we feel heartbroken, sick to our stomachs, punched in the gut.

That is the idea. And that's precisely what Jesus felt as He looked into the faces of people who were "harassed and helpless" —or, as another Bible translation puts it, "distressed and dispirited" (Matthew 9:36 NASB). To Him they resembled "sheep without a shepherd," meaning, they were vulnerable. Helpless. Clueless. Skittish and scared.

Just surveying the scene, Jesus felt His gut knot up. For all we know He got choked up.

• • •

The compassion of Christ, however, doesn't just fight back tears, shake its head, and say, How awful! It puts on its shoes, comes close, and whispers, How can I help? Matthew records that every time Jesus was filled with compassion, He did things . . . healed the sick (Matthew 14:14; 20:34) . . . fed the hungry (15:32). That's because compassion is active mercy, not passive pity.

Another thing about the Lord's compassion: It isn't just reserved for innocent victims—good people who have bad things happen to them. His heart also goes out to the guilty (see John 8).

• • •

More than a neat Bible concept, *compassion* is the great need of our world. Those loud neighbors, the surly coworker in the cubicle across from you, that annoying person on your Facebook feed . . . let's be honest, most days we'd like to give them the tax-collector treatment. But if we knew just a fraction of the hurts and hopelessness they're carrying, our hearts would shatter. As those who've experienced the compassion of Jesus, as His followers, we have the opportunity to extend His tender mercy.

Did you know our English word *compassion* comes from a Latin word that means "to suffer with"? Meaning, if you know someone today who is feeling harassed, helpless, or beaten down, maybe you could sit and suffer with them for thirty minutes today. Or possibly the person most in need of compassion right now is you. If so, if you're in trouble, or hurting, rest assured that Jesus sees. And trust in this truth: your situation moves Him deeply— *and* spurs Him to action.

28

TIRED

To be beaten down or fatigued—and in need of a recharge

Jacob's well was there; and Jesus, tired from the long walk, sat wearily
beside the well about noontime. (JOHN 4:6 NLT)

Exhaustion is now an accepted part of contemporary life.
It even has its own extensive vocabulary. People describe
themselves as

Bone-tired	Worn to a frazzle	Spent
Dog-tired	Running on empty	Shot
Pooped out	Ready to drop	Out of gas
Tuckered out	Bushed	Knackered
Wiped out	Beat	
Worn out	Sapped	

Maybe you're nodding (wearily) at that list. And—if you
could somehow find the energy—you'd like to grab and shake
some of those peppy people who are cheerfully buzzing around
you like a swarm of hyperactive hummingbirds.

What if I told you that Jesus knows a thing or two about being tired?

• • •

When John described Jesus slumping down at Jacob's well, he used
a word that suggested, in everyday Greek vernacular, a beating.

The vivid word picture is something like this: "You've been beat up by life, and you have nothing left." When you're in that weary place, can't you feel the gravitational pull of your couch or bed? And doesn't the simplest act—walking across the room to get your cell phone—feel like climbing Mount Everest?

This kind of beatdown can be physical (you've been doing back-breaking labor in the sun all day). It can be mental (you've got a bad case of brain strain from studying for and taking some intellectually rigorous exam). It can be emotional (you're stuck in a difficult, draining relationship with a toxic person). It can be spiritual too (you've been engaged in stressful ministry for an extended period—see 1 Kings 19—or trying with all your might to live as God intended).

● ● ●

"Me too." Or, "I've been there. I know what you're going through." That is what Jesus says to those who are utterly void of energy. Isn't that stunning? Because of the incarnation, God Almighty knows exactly what deep fatigue feels like, which explains why Jesus was always so adamant that His weary followers make and take time to rest (Matthew 11:28–30; Mark 6:31).

And notice one other thing. It wasn't just praying, boldness, and servanthood that Jesus modeled for His followers. He also modeled the God-honoring habit of taking a nap. On one particular jaunt across the Sea of Galilee (during a busy time of ministry), Jesus grabbed a cushion, found an empty spot in the boat, curled up, and caught forty winks (Mark 4:35–38).

● ● ●

There's no sin or shame in getting weary. We're human beings, not superheroes. If even our most technologically advanced machines eventually wear out, what makes us think that we shouldn't?

If you're weary today, that's okay. Maybe God is speaking to you through your exhaustion, "Stop! Lie down. Take a nap. I love it when you shine for me; I don't love it when you burn out."

29

TEACHER

One who helps others learn (comprehend and internalize)
important truths

You call me "Teacher" and "Lord," and rightly so, for that is what I am.

(JOHN 13:13)

There's nothing like a gifted *teacher.*

The best ones are consistently creative, occasionally shocking, always interesting. Due to their unpredictability and passion, we don't dare skip class—and when we're there we never look away. Good teachers make us think, make us work, and sometimes make us angry. Mostly, they make us thirsty to learn.

I once took a course in Bible study methods, taught by the legendary Howard Hendricks. Prof (as we called him) was spellbinding! Most of us were so inspired by the end of each class, we wanted to find a quiet place and dig into God's Word for the rest of the day!

I smile when I think of that experience. Then I shake my head as I think, *What must it have been like to hear Jesus teach?*

● ● ●

In the Bible a *teacher* is one who instructs others in the things of God. In Jewish culture during the time of Christ, teachers were known as *rabbis*. (This title of respect means "my superior one" or "my great one.") Revered rabbis were always followed by groups of eager students (*disciples*) who hoped to absorb a rabbi's knowledge and wisdom.

Jesus wasn't like the other religious teachers. The Gospels tell us that the crowds that heard Him teach were astonished, thunderstruck, because "he taught as one who had authority" (Matthew 7:28). Listeners found His words "amazing"—not in the sense of slick, but because they were weighty. We shouldn't be surprised since Jesus claimed that everything He taught came straight from God (John 7:16).

• • •

Wherever Jesus went—synagogues (Matthew 4:23), the temple (Matthew 21:23), the mountains (Matthew 5:1–2), the seashore (Mark 2:13)—He seized opportunities to teach. He told stories (aka *parables*)—sometimes funny, sometimes scandalous—from everyday life. And He often peppered His remarks with profound questions. In His teaching, Jesus was continually creative, always looking for ways to make God's truth understandable. He used life situations for object lessons (Luke 7:36–50). He used miracles as a springboard to help people grasp the bigger purposes of God (John 6).

If we could travel back in time and sit in on one of Jesus's teaching sessions, we'd be one hundred percent on the edge of our seats. At any moment, He might start blessing children, heal a sick person, rant against the Pharisees, or even conclude "class" with an all-you-can-eat dinner!

• • •

We don't have video or audio of Jesus instructing His followers, but we do have some of His teachings preserved for us in the New Testament.

Two questions: When's the last time you read the Gospels? Why not commit to reading the eighty-nine chapters of Matthew, Mark, Luke, and John over the next three months? That's only one chapter a day.

As you read, make David's prayer yours: "Teach me your way, LORD, that I may rely on your faithfulness; give me an undivided heart, that I may fear your name" (Psalm 86:11).

30

QUESTION

To query another with the purpose of stimulating thought
or eliciting desired information

They came to Capernaum; and when He was in the house,
He began to question them, "What were you discussing on the way?"
(MARK 9:33 NASB)

An unmissable aspect of the Gospels is how many questions they contain. People are constantly bombarding Jesus with questions. Not to be outdone, Jesus is shown continually firing questions at those around Him. In truth, His ministry was a lot like a nonstop, two-way press conference.

Why all the *questions*?

• • •

Several words are translated *question* in the New Testament. The most common one means to inquire, seek, or ask. It's the idea of interrogating.

Many of Jesus's enemies asked Him loaded questions. They were forever hoping to trap Him, to get Him in hot water, no matter how He responded. Sometimes Christ ignored His questioners (Luke 23:9). On other occasions, He turned the tables, answering their trick questions with even harder questions of His own, leaving them mumbling and staring sheepishly at the ground (Luke 20:40).

What about all the questions Jesus asked His disciples? (In his book *Jesus Is the Question*, Martin Copenhaver lists more than three hundred questions asked by Jesus in the Gospels!) Here's what we can say for sure: The One who came to seek and save the lost (Luke 19:10) used questions not to humiliate, but to illuminate and liberate.

● ● ●

New discoveries in the field of neuroscience reveal that good questions both engage and influence us. In a very real way questions hijack our attention. If I were to ask you, "Where would you like to go on your next vacation?" for a few moments at least—maybe longer if you lapsed into a daydream—you'd be unable to concentrate on anything else. (Of course, now I feel the need to say, "Come back! Forget vacations. Focus on these last few sentences!")

Research further shows that merely being asked about our future intentions has a way of influencing our future behavior.

No wonder Jesus, the ultimate teacher, asked so many piercing questions!

● ● ●

A good question carefully pondered can serve as a diagnostic tool. It can also be a catalyst for real change.

Here's a good exercise for followers of Jesus. For each of the next seven days, spend seven minutes mulling over these seven questions of Christ. Watch what happens in your heart.

1. "Who do you say that I am?" (Mark 8:27, 29 NASB)
2. "Can all your worries add a single moment to your life?" (Matthew 6:27 NLT)
3. "Why do you see the speck that is in your brother's eye, but do not notice the log that is in your own eye?" (Matthew 7:3 ESV)

4. "You of little faith, why are you so afraid?" (Matthew 8:26)
5. "What do you want me to do for you?" (Matthew 20:32 NASB)
6. "If I am telling you the truth, why don't you believe me?" (John 8:46)
7. "Do you love me?" (John 21:16)

31

PARABLE

A short, memorable story that has a dual meaning

Jesus spoke all these things to the crowd in parables; he did not say
anything to them without using a parable. (MATTHEW 13:34)

Speaker #1 is smart and well prepared. He launches into his
talk, energetically offering a wealth of practical information. Still, after a few minutes, all his facts and quotes and stats
and excellent points start blurring together. You struggle to track
with him; you fight the urge to check your phone.

Speaker #2 opens by telling about a job she had back in college
working at the city morgue . . . with a paraplegic coroner . . . who
was a Holocaust survivor. Her entire presentation you're leaning forward, hanging on her every word.

This highlights the truth that every good communicator
knows: Lectures can fill our heads, but it's stories that grab
our hearts.

Which helps explain why Jesus taught in *parables.*

• • •

The word *parable* literally means (in Greek) to "throw two things
alongside each other in order to compare them." In a broad sense,

a parable can be as concise as a proverb (see Luke 4:23) or a quick, one-sentence illustration (see Mark 13:28). Typically, the parables Jesus told were stories—metaphorical, short, always comparing everyday earthly experiences (a wedding celebration, a real-estate transaction, an agricultural venture, a search for something lost, etc.) to spiritual realities. Sometimes funny, often shocking, the parables of Jesus were always intended to get a reaction, to get people thinking, to linger in the heart.

If you've got a Bible that puts everything Jesus said in red ink, know this: His parables make up about a third of all those scarlet words. Jesus told a *lot* of stories.

• • •

Bible scholars have never agreed on how to interpret the parables of Jesus. Some argue that they have fanciful, allegorical meanings. Others insist they be viewed through a strict historical lens (in the unique context of first-century Jewish culture).

Here's what we can say for sure: If the parables leave *you* scratching your head, at least you're not alone. Even Jesus's original followers had to ask for help in grasping their meaning (Matthew 13:36; Mark 4:10; Luke 8:9).

And when they asked the Lord *why* He told so many stories to the masses (Matthew 13:10–17; Mark 4:11–12; Luke 8:10), His answer was stunning. Essentially He said He used parables to reveal divine truth to those who were hungry for it, and to hide such truth from those who weren't really interested.

• • •

Warning: The parables of Jesus are subversive. Once you've read them, there's no going back. They will linger and loiter in your conscience. They will annoy you and mess with you in all the best, most necessary ways.

When's the last time you read the parable of the lost son[*] (Luke 15:11–32)? Before you close your eyes tonight, read it again, slowly . . . carefully . . . prayerfully. Or reread the parable of the good Samaritan (Luke 10:25–37). You don't need a theology degree to get Jesus's point, I promise.

---

[*] Some have suggested that this famous story is really about *two* lost sons. The older son, without leaving home, was also far from his father.

32

LORD

A title of authority and respect that can refer to a
divine or human master, ruler, or owner

Why do you call me, "Lord, Lord," and do not do what I say? (LUKE 6:46)

When a police officer signals for us to pull over, we comply immediately. The same holds true when a coach yells, "Do it again!" or the boss buzzes to say tersely, "My office—ten minutes," or a teacher snaps, "See me after class."

When authority figures give us directives, we hop to it, no questions asked.

All of which makes one question of Jesus especially compelling, "Why do you call me, 'Lord, Lord,' and do not do what I say?"

• • •

In New Testament times, *Lord* was sometimes just a form of polite address—like saying "sir" (Matthew 13:27). More often it meant master (Matthew 6:24), owner (Luke 19:33; Galatians 4:1), or one with unrestricted authority (like a king or ruler).

In the early church, the term was reserved exclusively for Christ. When the angel announced the good news of the birth of Jesus to a group of startled shepherds, he identified Him as "a Savior . . . the Messiah, the Lord" (Luke 2:11). Thus we see *Lord* closely associated with the idea that Jesus was the long-awaited Savior, the King of the Jews.

After the resurrection, *Lord* came to mean even more to Christians—it suggested that Jesus Christ was, in fact, divine. To speak of Jesus as Lord was to acknowledge Him—not the Roman emperor or any other ruler—as the ultimate authority in life. * Inherent in addressing Jesus in this way is the idea, "And because you are Lord, you have every right to command me."

●　●　●

Lord isn't a term to use lightly. (Honestly? Saying it ought to make our hearts arrhythmic and our heads woozy.) The title suggests a master-servant relationship—the idea that since Jesus paid the highest price for us (1 Corinthians 6:19–20), we belong to Him. Therefore, its use should include a glad willingness to humble ourselves and submit to His will.

In the language of the kingdom of God, *Lord* is short for, "Your wish is my command." The point being, we can't call Jesus *Lord* one minute and ignore Him the next.

●　●　●

With His pointed, haunting question, Jesus was essentially saying, "A relationship with me involves much more than name-dropping. It requires putting my words into practice" (Luke 6:47, 49).

That truth raises other questions. What are we going to do now? How are we going to live today? Will we merely say a lot of God words . . . or actually follow the one who is *Lord*? Try to *sound* religious . . . or truly submit?

Which will it be?

---

* Interestingly, the Greek word *kurios* (translated "Lord") was used as a stand-in for YHWH in the Septuagint (the Greek translation of the Hebrew Old Testament).

33

STOOPED

To crouch low

Again he stooped down and wrote on the ground. (JOHN 8:8)

Nobody ever lists *stooping* as a skill on a job application. It's not hard to see why.

"Don't stoop to their level!" is our way of urging others not to abandon their principles. (Sort of like the old warning against wrestling with a pig—because you'll both end up filthy, but only the pig will enjoy it.)

When we speak of someone "stooping to conquer," we mean the person has ulterior motives. He only assumes a lowly position in order to gain some selfish advantage.

When we lament, "How could they stoop so low?" we are expressing shock at an utter disregard for moral or ethical standards.

We cringe at the idea of stooping.

And then, lo and behold, we see Jesus doing it.

● ● ●

The story at the beginning of John 8 isn't found in the oldest, most reliable Greek manuscripts. Most Bible translations put a note to that effect in the margin, or they put the passage in italics or brackets. Nevertheless, most scholars agree that the story itself is authentic, that it certainly happened.

It features the Pharisees dragging an adulterous woman before Jesus and essentially asking Him, "What consequences should a person like this face?"

It was a trap, of course . . . an attempt to get Jesus to say something that would get Him in trouble with either the Romans or the masses. How did Jesus respond? He "stooped down and with His finger wrote on the ground" (John 8:6 NASB).

Stooped means exactly what we think. Christ bent low. He crouched down close to the earth.

• • •

Artistic depictions of this scene have this woman cowering against a wall, crumpled with her face in her hands, or face down in the dirt. None of these images seem far-fetched. In such a horrible, humiliating moment, who wouldn't be trying to climb under the ground?

Then Jesus stoops. Maybe by writing in the dust He was trying to divert the gaze of the crowd away from this disgraced woman to himself. In this posture, all eyes were suddenly riveted on Him . . . looking down on Him. (Meaning: Jesus knows, literally, what it's like to be "looked down upon.") It's a picture of humility, of the incarnation, of Christ's entire ministry, actually. Stooping next to a disgraced woman so she wouldn't feel alone. Crouching to wash feet (John 13:5). Bending over the sick (Luke 4:39). Leaning down to engage little kids. That's our stooping Savior . . . always descending, choosing the low place . . . in order to dole out grace . . . and lift up the downtrodden.

• • •

Read the whole story and marvel at the irony and beauty of it. The cold-hearted, self-righteous Pharisees unwittingly did this woman the greatest favor possible. They caught her at her lowest point and dragged her to Jesus. There in His humble presence, she found full forgiveness and a new life!

Her experience reminds us that our most shameful failures don't have to be endings. If they lead us to Jesus and His grace, they can be new beginnings. Corrie Ten Boom said it best, "There is no pit so deep that God is not deeper still."

34

BLIND

Unable to see physical or spiritual realities

Since the beginning of time it has never been heard that anyone opened
the eyes of a person born blind. (JOHN 9:32 NASB)

Jesus gravitated toward the visually impaired the way a house
flipper is drawn to fixer-uppers.

Christ the ophthalmologist . . . who knew?

The first gospel records two instances of Jesus healing sightless men by placing His hands on their eyes (Matthew 9:27–31;
20:29–34). In Bethsaida, He once *spit* on a blind man's eyes, then
added an extra touch to give the guy crystal clear, HD-quality
vision (Mark 8:22–26). Near Jericho, Christ changed the life
of one blind beggar by simply announcing, "Your faith has healed
you" (Mark 10:46–52). In Jerusalem, He opened the eyes of a man
who'd been blind his whole life by rubbing a mixture of saliva and
dust on the guy's defective peepers, then telling him to go wash
off in the Pool of Siloam (John 9).

All this, plus all the other times He restored sightless souls
in big crowds during special healing services (Matthew 15:29–31;
Luke 7:18–23).

• • •

In the Bible *blindness* is often physiological—the inability to see
physical realities. But the Scriptures also refer often to spiritual
blindness. Unbelievers are described as being blind to the truth

of God (2 Corinthians 4:4; 1 John 2:11). Those who reject God's light are said to live in darkness (John 3:19; 8:12).

An ironic—and tragic—case in point: Jesus labeled the religious leaders who opposed Him "blind guides" and observed, "If the blind lead the blind, both will fall into a pit" (Matthew 15:14). Apparently Jesus felt these men also had hearing issues, because in Matthew 23 He called them "blind guides! . . . blind fools! . . . blind men! . . . blind guides! . . . blind Pharisee!" (vv. 16, 17, 19, 24, 26).

Sigh. Because of their dark hearts they couldn't (or wouldn't) have recognized the truth if they had been staring at it. (And in truth that's exactly what—or whom—they *were* staring at.)

• • •

The ancient prophets declared that in the kingdom of God, the eyes of the blind would be opened (Isaiah 29:18; 35:5). Thus Jesus's frequent healings of the blind were signals, or signs, announcing His true identity as God's anointed. Through His words and works, Jesus was pleading with a vision-impaired world, "Come out of the darkness. Come to me and receive sight. I can turn the lights on in your heart. I can open your eyes. Let me show you what's true."

• • •

What is it that you can't see today?

God's purpose for your life?

The reason you're suffering?

Some truth about God's character—His love or grace or sovereignty?

A way out of your current predicament?

Since Jesus has compassion for those who can't see—and also the power to restore sight, let the cry of the blind man in Luke 18 be your cry: "Jesus, Son of David, have mercy on me! . . . Lord, I want to see" (vv. 38, 41).

35

POOR

To be destitute, without resources (whether material
or spiritual or social)

Looking at his disciples, he said: "Blessed are you who are poor,
for yours is the kingdom of God." (LUKE 6:20)

Some preachers have built big followings (and bigger fortunes) by making the gospel some version of this formula: "Give your money to God—or more specifically to *me*, God's servant— and He will bless you right back! He'll make *you* wealthy."

Never mind that the Gospels (a) show Jesus acquiring exactly zilch in terms of worldly wealth; and (b) record Him consistently speaking about the unexpected upside of poverty and the grave danger of riches (Luke 8:14; 12:15).

Jesus was born to young parents who were barely scraping by. How else do we explain the shocking circumstances of His birth? Why else would Mary and Joseph have offered a pauper's sacrifice—pigeons instead of the customary lamb (see Luke 2:22–24 and Leviticus 12:7–8)? A working-class carpenter (Mark 6:3) until the age of thirty (Luke 3:23), Jesus apparently spent the final three years of His life crashing with others (Matthew 8:20). The ultimate minimalist (Luke 12:33), He was constantly borrowing things. He bummed rides (via boat [see Luke 5:3] and donkey [see Matthew 21:1–7]). He borrowed sack lunches (John

6:9–11) and coins (Matthew 22:19). Even in death, He was still borrowing—a rich man's tomb (but only for the weekend).

• • •

The Greek word translated *poor* is related to a verb that means "to bow or crouch." The image behind this word is that of a kneeling beggar who seeks handouts.

In the Bible, poverty can take different forms. It can mean financial destitution (not having adequate food, clothing, shelter, income [see Matthew 19:21]). It can take the form of social neediness (being an unwelcome outsider or outcast). Or it can mean spiritual bankruptcy (such as when Jesus talked about those who are "poor in spirit" in Matthew 5:3).

Whatever the case, being poor means you have nothing to offer. Without help from someone else with ample resources, you won't make it.

• • •

Here's why Jesus said that poverty can be a hidden blessing and wealth can be so dangerous.

As long as we have assets of any kind (financial, physical, social, etc.), we tell ourselves we can deal with whatever problems arise. When our portfolios include savings, good health, abilities, reputation, connections, and so on, we feel safe. And when we feel like we're insulated from trouble, we tend to think, *Who needs God?*

On the other hand, knowing you're poor drives you to your knees. When I can't write a check or call in a favor to make a problem go away, I become desperate and dependent. I end up humbled.

And that's a blessing, not a curse, because God gives grace to the humble (James 4:6). Instead of relying on meager, worldly assets (that can disappear in a moment), I get to enjoy "the boundless riches of Christ" (Ephesians 3:8).

• • •

The problem with the preachers who fixate on wealth isn't that they go too far; it's that they don't go far enough. They're looking around when they should be looking up. Why settle for $1,500 sneakers, 10,000-square-foot mansions, or fancy Learjets, when Jesus has so much more for us?

WOMEN

Females, as distinct from males

But all those who knew him, including the women who had followed him from Galilee, stood at a distance, watching these things. (LUKE 23:49)

Here's the nicest way we can say it: Judeo-Christian religion has not always been kind to women.

For too many years and in too many quarters, women have been considered inferior to men. Perhaps the most infamous example is the prayer from the Jewish Talmud that goes, "Blessed are you, Lord, for not making me a woman." Sadly, even the revered Christian theologian Augustine taught, in so many words, that men are more like God than women are.

Thoughts like these are bad enough. The actions they've prompted are even worse. Who would dispute—with a straight face—that women have been marginalized, silenced, and treated as second-class believers for much of church history?

Not surprisingly, many—especially in the last fifty years—have concluded the Christian faith is fundamentally antiwoman.

Jesus would say, "Whoa! Not so fast."

• • •

The Greek word translated *woman* in the New Testament gives us our English word *gynecology*. It refers to a female person.

While it's true that Jewish culture at the time of Christ was male dominated . . . it's also true that Jesus ignored, rejected, and reversed many of His culture's gender biases and practices:

- He denounced the objectification of women (Matthew 5:28).
- He engaged women publicly—something unheard of in His day (John 4:7–27).
- He invariably treated women with respect, honor, and compassion (Luke 7:12–13; 8:48).
- He stood up for women who were being used and mistreated (John 8:1–11).
- He alleviated the suffering of women (Matthew 9:20–22; Mark 5:34; Luke 13:12).
- He welcomed women into His group of followers—something other rabbis did not do. (And in many instances they proved to be more loyal students than His male disciples!)
- When He rose from the dead, He appeared first to some of His female followers (Matthew 28:1; Mark 16:1; Luke 23:55–24:5; John 20:1). This is fascinating since, according to Josephus and the Talmud, a woman's testimony was considered less reliable than a man's.

• • •

In a culture that largely treated women as an afterthought, Luke 13 gives us a radical snapshot of Christ. While teaching in a synagogue, Jesus noticed a woman who was crippled, bent over like a pretzel. A demonic spirit had kept her trapped in such a state for eighteen years. Calling her forward, Jesus said, "Woman, you are set free" (Luke 13:12).

Instantly, she was healed, delivered by the original and ultimate women's liberator.

• • •

If you know people who have rejected the Christian faith because of how Christians (and churches) have viewed and treated women, encourage them to read back through the Gospels and see just how pro-woman Jesus was (and is).

37

CHILDREN

Sons and daughters; offspring

He called a little child to him, and placed the child among them. And he said: "Truly I tell you, unless you change and become like little children, you will never enter the kingdom of heaven." (MATTHEW 18:2–3)

How different was childhood in first-century Israel from the experience of modern children in Western culture?

Put it this way: No Jewish parents in AD 28 were arranging the entire family schedule around little Samuel's athletic endeavors or making a gigantic, public fuss over baby Miriam's first tooth, poop, step, or sleepover.

To be clear, children in ancient Israel were considered a distinct blessing, a wonderful gift from God (Psalm 127). From a utilitarian standpoint, the more kids—especially sons—the better (since child labor laws weren't yet a thing).

Jewish culture valued children, but it surely wasn't kid-centric. Which made Jesus's attitude toward, and comments about, children somewhat shocking.

• • •

Two primary Greek words are translated *children* in the New Testament and are used to convey either the broad idea of offspring (of any age or either sex), or more specifically younger children (infants, older boys and girls). The words are sometimes used figuratively as terms of endearment (for example, "son" in Matthew 9:2, and "my children" in 3 John 4).

When parents sought out Jesus to pray for and bless their newborns, rug-rats, and toddlers, He got indignant—not at the parents, but at His own disciples who were trying to shoo the parents away (Mark 10:13–16)! For a few minutes, or a few hours—the gospel writers don't say—Jesus was like a star athlete signing autographs. Except that it was little hearts He was writing on with His tender touch and love. His modus operandi where kids were concerned? "Let the little children come to me, and do not hinder them, for the kingdom of heaven belongs to such as these" (Matthew 19:14; see also Luke 18:16).

• • •

Kids weren't a photo-op for Jesus. He didn't hug on babies to boost His approval ratings. Funny, but while most religious teachers in Christ's day were much too busy "doing the Lord's work" to stop and acknowledge children, the Lord saw engaging children as a big part of His work!

Jesus issued terrifying warnings to anyone who would cause children to stumble (Mark 9:42). He made an intriguing comment about children having guardian angels (Matthew 18:10). He also demonstrated enormous compassion for parents with kids in trouble (Luke 8:41–42).

• • •

Mostly, Jesus held up kids as a picture of what it means to be a true child of God. "Truly I tell you, unless you change and become like little children, you will never enter the kingdom of heaven" (Matthew 18:3).

He was referring to the way kids are utterly dependent . . . and authentic about their neediness. When a child is in trouble or scared, he or she runs instinctively into the arms of the nearest parent.

Ask one hundred people to complete the sentence, "Children are _____," and you'll hear responses like "expensive," "a pain," "a gift," "funny," "a blessing," "a lot of work," "our future."

Jesus might very well say, "my favorite."

38

SINNER

One who—in terms of pleasing God—falls short and is thus deemed to be a spiritual failure

Why do you eat and drink with tax collectors and sinners? (LUKE 5:30)

What's the worst label you can stick on a person?

In our pluralistic culture, it depends on assorted factors, doesn't it? Conservative, liberal . . . rich, poor . . . atheist, evangelical . . . tree hugger, climate change denier—all of these can be hurled with a sneer (and often are).

In first-century Jewish culture, the worst names you could call a person were *tax collector* and *sinner.*

• • •

Tax collector is self-explanatory. (These were Jews who made a nice living—in many cases, a fortune—by extracting money from their countrymen, giving a certain percentage to the hated Roman government and pocketing the rest.)

Sinner was the broad term given to irreligious Jews. The Greek word translated "sinner" means "one who fails to hit the mark." Thus, a sinner was a person deemed a spiritual failure. He wasn't good at keeping the Mosaic law, knew he wasn't, and in many cases wasn't even trying anymore. Or she was tired of pretending to have it all together, and convinced she would never be accept-able to God, so she just walked away from it all. Attend services at the synagogue? No way. Offer sacrifices at the temple in Jeru-salem? Are you kidding?

Because sinners didn't follow the rules, the "moral majority" ostracized them. They were seen as outcasts, far from God, scum, to put it bluntly.*

●　●　●

The response of Jesus to sinners is one of the biggest surprises in the Bible. We would think God in the flesh would surely find sinners repulsive—and let them have it.

But the only thing Jesus let them have was grace and truth! Far from avoiding them (like the religious leaders did), Jesus sought them out (Matthew 9:11). He welcomed them (Luke 15:2) and dined with them (Luke 19:7). As a result, the irreligious crowd flocked to Jesus (Matthew 9:10) like bugs to a light bulb! (Proba-bly because they knew their lives were such a mess—and His heart overflowed grace.) In time Jesus became known as "a friend of tax collectors and sinners" (Matthew 11:19; Luke 7:34). (And the religious leaders didn't mean this as a compliment!)

Why sinners? Because they were His mission. Jesus came to earth to call sinners to repentance (Mark 2:17; Luke 5:32)—and He said that every time one does repent, heaven throws a party for the ages (Luke 15:7, 10)!

●　●　●

Jesus's interactions with sinners reveal a staggering truth. Only one group of people will ever taste God's grace—those who real-ize they are spiritual failures.

---

* "Why do you eat and drink with such scum?" is how Luke 5:30 is rendered in the New Living Translation.

The prerequisite for membership in God's forever family? Grasping the truth that you're a sinner, a spiritual disaster.

Until you realize "That's me!" you can't get into the club. When you do, you're ready to accept Christ's invitation to the party that will never end.

39

HEART

The central essence of human personality

These people honor me with their lips, but their hearts are far from me.

(MATTHEW 15:8)

I remember my small group one night wrestling at length with the question, What does God want *most* from us?

It was a lively discussion. We flipped through the Good Book for a while, batting verses around like badminton birdies. Before we called it a day, we decided that God doesn't merely want us to be nice, or moral, or to engage in various spiritual practices. We also concluded that being good parents and voting in a certain way are not His primary concerns.

According to Jesus, more than our money or our compliance or our service, the Lord wants our hearts.

• • •

More than 150 times in the New Testament we find the Greek word *kardia* translated "heart." (Yep, this is where we get our word *cardiology*.) And yet, when the Bible speaks of the heart, it almost never means the blood-pumping organ in our chests. Instead, it's referring to our immaterial, innermost being—where we feel, yes, but also where we think and choose. In short, the Bible sees the heart as the control center of one's life. No wonder wise old Solomon declared, "Above all else, guard your heart, for everything you do flows from it" (Proverbs 4:23).

In Matthew 15:8, Jesus was looking at a group of people who were checking every religious box. He shook His head sadly and quoted God's words to and through the prophet Isaiah, "Their hearts are far from me." Ouch! More than a flurry of good deeds and spiritual-sounding words, the Lord wants our hearts.

Sit down and ponder that staggering truth. Jesus wants to make His home in your heart (Ephesians 3:17), fill it with His love (1 John 4:19), then watch you find ultimate joy in loving Him back and loving others with everything you've got (Mark 12:29–31).

• • •

Whether you're daydreaming (again) about some lifelong dream . . . worrying about a wayward child . . . nervously waiting for medical test results . . . smarting over the cruel comment of a co-worker . . . or getting choked up over a scene so beautiful it takes your breath away—all of that involves your heart. That's the stuff of life. And whether it's good, bad, or blah, Jesus wants to be right there with you in the middle of it all. That's because He wants your heart. He wants you.

• • •

No wonder Jesus talked so much about the heart—about having a pure heart (Matthew 5:8), about how our hearts can become dull (13:15) and hard (19:8), about how our hearts naturally attach to whatever it is we value most in life (6:21).

Right now is a perfect time to let the Great Cardiologist examine your heart. And when He does, if you realize it's not exactly oozing with love, how about borrowing this honest prayer from Teresa of Avila: "Lord, I don't love you. I don't even want to love you. But I want to want to love you."

40

SAW

The past tense of the verb that means to notice, to perceive, to "get" a situation

When Jesus saw him lying there and learned that he had been in this condition for a long time, he asked him, "Do you want to get well?"

(JOHN 5:6)

Often when preachers and writers tackle this verse, they focus on the strange words of Jesus. Who asks a chronically sick person, "Do you want to get well?" The question seems tone deaf at best, cruel at worst. (In truth, it's a brilliant question—but that's not our focus here.)

Instead, look at something else. Pay attention to the common, easy-to-overlook phrase "Jesus saw." Eighteen separate times in the Gospels,* Matthew, Mark, Luke, and John use that phrase, noting how Jesus saw certain people or assorted things.

• • •

In this instance (John 5), Jesus showed up at Bethesda, a pool just north of the Jerusalem temple. Why there? Why that particular day? A study of the Gospels shows that Jesus was always intentional and purposeful, always in sync with the Father, always

---

* This number is based on the NIV translation.

committed to carrying out the Father's will. Jesus didn't do anything randomly.

He went to Bethesda, a place that must have resembled a primitive, outdoor ER waiting room—sick and broken people sprawled everywhere. And there, "Jesus saw" a man who'd been paralyzed for almost four decades! It wasn't a mindless glance. The verb *saw* suggests that Jesus took notice of the man, stared intently at him, perceiving his situation. Then, in the place with the name that means "house of mercy," Jesus gave a helpless, hopeless man the mercy of a lifetime.

● ● ●

It's common—and awful—to feel invisible, isn't it? To feel like no one sees your pain—no one sees *you*. Your world is unraveling, and busy, preoccupied people—sometimes even dear friends—blow right past, oblivious, distracted.

But, oh, what it does for our hearts when someone notices. To have someone stop, look you in the eyes, and say, "I see what you're going through. I'm so sorry. I'm here for you. What do you need?" What a priceless gift!

● ● ●

The phrase "Jesus saw" reminds us that Jesus was (and still is) wonderfully observant. He's a noticer, always aware of His surroundings, always picking up on nonverbal clues. Not sure about that? Read the Gospels and note how consistently Christ "read the room," observing the restlessness of crowds, the faith or spiritual hunger of certain people, the sadness or fear lurking in assorted hearts.

"Jesus saw" is good news for two reasons: (1) It means He sees all the junk and chaos we're up against. ("The eyes of the LORD are everywhere," Proverbs 15:3 assures us.) He's constantly monitoring our lives (and He doesn't get distracted). And (2) it means

He can help those of us who aren't quite so observant to become more aware and more other-focused.

Imagine if we got so good at seeing that no one ever felt invisible around us.

41

READY

To be committed and on standby

Because of the crowd he told his disciples to have a small boat ready for him,
to keep the people from crowding him. (MARK 3:9)

Big-name politicians, legendary musicians and movie stars—even famous athletes—often use bodyguards to shield them from the masses. When fans get too rowdy or paparazzi get too close, these security teams often hustle celebrities into waiting limousines and whisk them away.

Believe it or not, Jesus had a similar system in place back in the first century. He drew huge, enthusiastic crowds. And people were always trying to touch Him. In Galilee—especially around the Sea of Galilee*—Jesus made sure His entourage kept a small boat ready nearby.

Sometimes He'd use the boat as a kind of floating platform. His disciples would push the boat out into the water a few yards, and from there He'd continue teaching the crowds (Matthew 13:2; Mark 4:1). On other occasions, He'd use the boat to cross the lake.

● ● ●

"Have a small boat ready" was Christ's command. And what a fascinating instruction!

---

* The Sea of Galilee is only about eight miles wide (at its widest point) and thirteen miles long; it's actually a freshwater lake, and was sometimes called Chinnereth, Gennesaret, or Tiberias.

The word *ready* is a common word meaning literally "to remain with." When used of people it carried the idea of loyalty. If you were *ready*, it meant you were dedicated and focused. You were on standby, prepared to swing into action if need be.

Maybe the crowds would be orderly and respectful, and the boat wouldn't be needed. But it was there and available, just in case. It was *ready*. Sort of like Jesus was always ready to do whatever would please His Father in heaven (John 8:29).

• • •

In 1986 archaeologists digging along the northwest shore of the Sea of Galilee unearthed a fishing boat that they dated to the first century. Roughly 27 feet long and 7.5 feet wide, it's exactly the kind of boat that commercial fishermen like Peter, Andrew, James, and John would have used.

There's no evidence that this boat is, in any way, connected to Jesus, much less that it's *the* boat referred to in Mark 3. But one never knows.

One undeniable truth: The boat stands ready for tourists to view at the Yigal Allon Galilee Boat Museum in Ginosar, Israel.

• • •

In one sense, everybody is ready for something. Ready for the weekend. Ready to order. Ready to rumble. Maybe you're ready to go, ready to pop the question, ready to make a change.

The big question—the question being put to us by a nondescript, inanimate New Testament boat—is, Are we ready for Jesus to use us—for whatever purposes He deems, and whenever and wherever He wants?

Before it's a question of availability, it's a question of commitment.

42

AMAZED

To be in a state of astonishment, to be filled with wonder

The men were amazed and asked, "What kind of man is this? Even the winds and the waves obey him!" (MATTHEW 8:27)

I s any adjective more amazing* than the word *amazing*?
A coworker can't stop talking about that "amazing" new series on Netflix, and the Facebook pictures of your friend's vacation to Santorini look pretty amazing too. (Don't forget your brother's amazing new car, those amazing cinnamon rolls your daughter made on Saturday, or your uncle's amazing recovery from a terrible car wreck last year.)

Perhaps we shouldn't be amazed to find out that the word *amazed* pops up over and over in the life of Christ.

• • •

Several Greek words get translated *amazed* in the New Testament. The general meaning is "to be astonished or filled with wonder and surprise." True amazement is more than being impressed. It's being wide-eyed, slack-jawed, tongue-tied.

---

* Or more overused? Perhaps the word *awesome*? (It's amazingly overused too.)

Jesus had this effect everywhere He went. The masses were constantly amazed by His words (Matthew 7:28; Luke 4:36) and the religious leaders at His learning (John 7:15). The disciples were thunderstruck by His obvious authority over raging storms (Matthew 8:27) and raging demons (Matthew 9:33–43). As He healed the sick (Matthew 12:22; Luke 5:17–26) and raised up those who had been paralyzed (Mark 2:12), Jesus left jaws hanging open all over Israel.

• • •

There are two instances in the Gospels when Jesus was described not as being amazing but as being amazed. Once was when He visited His hometown of Nazareth. After the many astonishing things He'd said and done, His own neighbors "took offense at him" (Mark 6:3). Mark tragically reports that Jesus departed, "amazed at their lack of faith" (Mark 6:6).

On another occasion, Jesus was approached by a Roman centurion, who respectfully requested healing for his sick servant. "I'm not asking you to make a house call—I don't deserve that," the man essentially said. "But just say the word, and I know my servant will be healed long distance" (Matthew 8:8).

Matthew records that Jesus was amazed by this, and that He turned to those following Him and praised the centurion's remarkable faith.

• • •

The moral of these two stories is this: If we're going to amaze Jesus, it's better to do it by having deep faith than by having no faith.

Though we often toss around the word *amazing*, it's rare that we stop and surrender to genuine amazement. The miracle of a twinkling night sky. The mystery of a newborn child sound asleep on your chest. The precious gift of a long-term friendship.

The wondrous promise that a good God sees you at this very moment, loves you, and has promised to be with you forever.

Allow yourself to be amazed by some blessing of God before your head hits the pillow tonight (or, failing that, after it does).

43

FAITH

Confidence, belief, or trust

"Where is your faith?" he asked his disciples. (LUKE 8:25)

For some, faith is like a priceless gem or rare coin. They bring it out on occasion to show (read "impress" or "dazzle") select people. Usually, however, they keep it "locked away for safekeeping." In this way of thinking, faith is a precious asset to have, offering long-term security . . . but it's not exactly something that makes a difference in one's everyday life.

For others, faith is like a fancy treadmill or exercise bike. When utilized, it can (and does) enhance life, but most weeks (months? years?) it sits idly over in the corner, buried under all the dusty stuff that has been piled atop it.

For Jesus, faith is everything. It's the irreducible minimum of the spiritual life, the *sine qua non*, the be all–end all. In down-to-earth (or at least down-to-Texas) terms, *faith* is the whole enchilada.

● ● ●

In the Bible, *faith* means trust or belief in who God is and what God says. It conveys the idea of confidence, dependence, or reliance.

About twenty-five times in the Gospels, we see Jesus speaking about faith. (This doesn't count all the other times He used related verbs like *believe* or *believes*.) And what exactly did Jesus say about trusting God?

Lots. He told people to have faith (Mark 11:22), told them that faith is what saves them (Luke 7:50). He asked His followers hard questions like "Where is your faith?" (Luke 8:25) and "Do you still have no faith?" (Mark 4:40). He chided people with "little faith" (Matthew 6:30; 8:26; 14:31; 16:8; 17:20) and praised those with "great faith" (Matthew 8:10; 15:28; Luke 7:9).

He told Peter, "I have prayed . . . that your faith may not fail" (Luke 22:32).

• • •

Why is faith so significant to Jesus? To answer that question we need to ponder other questions: How was humanity's relationship with God shattered in the first place? How did the world get broken?

Answer: Through a failure of faith. Sin (and all its grim consequences) entered the picture only after Adam and Eve refused to trust God. Therefore, doesn't it makes sense that Christ the Savior would come into our world to (a) show us that God is, indeed, worthy of our trust; and (b) call us to believe.

• • •

Linguistically, the word *faith* is a noun. Actually and practically, faith insists that we treat it like a verb. The faith Jesus produces in His followers isn't content to languish in our hearts like some inert concept, some vapid list of spiritual ideas, or some precious jewel locked away in a vault. Jesus-pleasing faith means active trust.

Though faith begins in the heart, it always leads to action. Otherwise, how would Jesus "see" the faith of people (Matthew 9:2; Mark 2:5; Luke 5:20)?

One last thing . . . if you're not exactly oozing faith right now, you can always do what the apostles did: ask the Lord to increase your faith (Luke 17:5).

44

SABBATH

The seventh day of the week, designated
by God as a day for rest

For the Son of Man is Lord of the Sabbath. (MATTHEW 12:8)

Reading the Gospels, we can't help but notice the Jewish religious leaders getting furious with Jesus for doing seemingly good things:

- Allowing His hungry followers to pick and eat a few kernels of wheat (Matthew 12:1–8)
- Restoring a man with a withered hand (Matthew 12:9–14)
- Healing a woman from a disfiguring disease (Luke 13:10–17)
- Curing a man of dropsy (Luke 14:1–6)
- Healing an invalid at the pool of Bethesda (John 5:1–15)
- Restoring a blind man's sight (John 9:1–14)

Why would such helpful actions trigger so much rage? Because Jesus did them on the *Sabbath*.

• • •

Many Christians wrongly think *Sabbath* is a synonym for Sunday. In actuality, the word *Sabbath* comes from a Hebrew word that means "to cease." (In Jewish culture the Sabbath begins right after sundown on Friday and ends at sunset on Saturday.)

According to Genesis 2:2–3, God instituted the Sabbath after He finished creating the world. Ponder that. God Almighty rested —not in the sense that He was tired and needed a nap—but in order to enjoy the work of His hands. (He later told Moses that He found the day refreshing—see Exodus 31:17.)

Later, in commanding the fledgling nation of Israel to observe Sabbath (Exodus 20:8–11), God was offering His people a great gift. Sabbath is God saying, "Enough! Stop working. Take time out from the hectic business—and busyness—of your life. I want you resting, relaxing, reflecting on what's true, remembering my goodness, and rejoicing. For this day, don't worry about *doing*. Just *be*. Be with me. And be glad in the good life I have given you."

* * *

Leave it to well-meaning religious people to totally miss God's point. By the time of Christ, the Jewish religious leaders couldn't get beyond the "Stop working!" part of the Sabbath. They actually devised an elaborate list of thirty-nine kinds of work that they saw as forbidden. (They even had arguments over whether it was permissible to wear one's false teeth on the Sabbath day!)

Then, even worse, these self-appointed Sabbath-police spent their time hunting for Sabbath violators. And so the Sabbath became a headache.

The irony of it all? By constantly obsessing and arguing over what constitutes *carrying* a burden on the Sabbath, they turned the whole day into one giant burden!

* * *

"Do I *have* to celebrate Sabbath?" is asking the wrong question. Better to ask, "How much more fulfilling would my life be if I earmarked one day out of seven for rest and reflection, replenishment and rejuvenation?"

I won't lie . . . resisting the powerful urge to *be productive* and *accomplish more* takes great faith. We worry, *Will there be enough time to get everything done?*

By the gift of the Sabbath God says, "Absolutely! You can go off-duty because you can trust me. While you recharge and relax, I'm still God and I'm still at work."

Going hard 24/7?

The Bible suggests 24/6 is more than enough.

45

TEMPLE

A dwelling place for a deity—and thus a place where
humans could encounter and worship that deity

Jesus answered them, "Destroy this temple, and I will raise it again in
three days." They replied, "It has taken forty-six years to build this temple,
and you are going to raise it in three days?" But the temple he had spoken
of was his body. (JOHN 2:19–21)

When God made the Israelites His covenant people at Sinai,
He gave them plans for something called a tabernacle.
This was—literally—a glorified tent. It housed, among other
things, the ark of the covenant—that sacred, golden box contain-
ing the stone tablets upon which God had inscribed His law.

Shockingly, God condescended to fill this portable worship
center with His majestic glory (see Exodus 40). All the years of
Israel's wilderness wandering, the tabernacle was a comforting
reminder, a powerful symbol of God's presence with His people.

Once Israel settled in the promised land, King Solomon up-
graded the nation's primary worship facility. He built a lavish
temple in Jerusalem, using the finest stone and timbers around.
When it was complete, God manifested His presence there—
to the great awe and joy of all the people (1 Kings 8:10–13). This
magnificent structure stood for more than 350 years, until the
Babylonian armies of Nebuchadnezzar destroyed it in 587 BC (see
2 Kings 25:8–12). Talk about national despair!

But God is faithful, even when His people aren't. In 539 BC the exiled Jews were granted permission to return to Jerusalem and rebuild their temple. Another four hundred–plus years passed and King Herod the Great ordered an extreme temple makeover.

This was the temple in which Jesus was presented as a baby (see Luke 2:21–38). It's where His parents found Him (at age twelve) dialoguing with the Jewish scribes (Luke 2:41–30). It's the place Jesus labeled "my Father's house."

●   ●   ●

When the boy had grown up, He returned to the temple for Passover and caused an unforgettable ruckus (John 2:13–17). Horrified at all the merchants and money changers who had set up shop in the temple courts, Jesus fashioned a makeshift whip, and became a one-man wrecking crew. Flipping over tables and flinging money boxes left and right, He chased them all away!

When asked to provide some miraculous sign to demonstrate His authority to take such radical action, Jesus uttered His famous statement, "Destroy this temple, and I will raise it again in three days."

●   ●   ●

The Jewish religious leaders scoffed at this statement. Herod's remodeling project had taken nearly five decades! But John says that "the temple he had spoken of was his body" (John 2:21).

Don't miss the significance of this. If a temple is where God Almighty dwells in His glory . . . if it's a place where imperfect people can approach a holy God and find forgiveness and fullness of joy (Psalm 16:11), then Jesus was saying, in effect, "You don't need a building anymore. You need me."

●   ●   ●

Jesus is the living temple of God. He's where the glory of God is manifested! We come to the Father by coming to Jesus (John 14:6). No wonder John says in another place, speaking of Jesus, "We have seen his glory, the glory of the Father's one and only Son" (John 1:14 NLT).

46

PHARISEES

A Jewish religious political party that often
clashed with Jesus

When the Pharisees saw this, they asked his disciples, "Why does your
teacher eat with tax collectors and sinners?" (MATTHEW 9:11)

Bet you know some folks like this . . .

They've got God figured out. They know exactly how
you should live (and they're more than happy to tell you). They're
suspicious—even contemptuous—of anyone who disagrees with
them. They're into how things *look* (and more importantly, how
they look). They're obsessed with rules—the more the better. They
love being in charge, love loopholes (that exempt them from their
own rules), love arguing, love being praised for their piety.

Go along with them, and this group will treat you well. Cross
them or dismiss them at your own peril.

In the time of Christ, these people were called the *Pharisees*.

• • •

By the time of Jesus, the Pharisees, a mostly middle-class religious
and political party, had been active in Israel for nearly two hundred
years. Their roots date back to the time when Israel was under the
thumb of Greece—and Greek culture and philosophy were start-
ing to infiltrate Jewish life.

The word *Pharisee* comes from an Aramaic word meaning separated. As their name suggests, this group sought to avoid association with pagans (Greeks or Romans—or even fellow Jews who didn't embrace their complicated interpretations of the Mosaic law). Rather than concern for such "wayward" people, they had contempt for them.

Not all the Pharisees were prigs. Some were good-hearted and honorable—you'd have wanted to have them as neighbors. Many, however, were filled with a holier-than-thou attitude. They saw themselves as the guardians of public morality. As self-appointed spiritual and cultural policemen (and judges), they viewed everything and everybody through a critical lens. And in their devotion to the law (or, more accurately, to their scribal interpretations of it), they fell into the devilish trap of thinking they were actually earning God's approval.

●　●　●

The Pharisees clashed constantly with Jesus. Why? Because He saw through—and challenged— their twisted, soul-killing interpretations of the Mosaic law. He called them on their hypocrisy. What's more, instead of shunning and shaming tax collectors and "sinners," He welcomed and befriended them (Matthew 11:19; Luke 7:34)! No wonder religious outsiders flocked to Him! Rather than the Pharisaical message, "Clean up your act, and *then* I'll accept you," Jesus graciously accepted social outcasts and moral failures by grace, with no strings or fine print attached. Such unconditional love made them *want* to change (see Luke 19:1–10)!

●　●　●

The Pharisaical spirit lives on. But it doesn't have to live in your heart. Let Matthew 23 be like an MRI of your soul. Ask the Spirit of God to use the words of Jesus there to show you if there are Pharisaical attitudes or actions in your life. If there are, confess them. Turn from them. The world doesn't need more Pharisees. It needs more Jesus.

47

PRAY

Opening one's heart—and perhaps even
one's mouth—to God

This, then, is how you should pray: "Our Father in heaven . . ."
(MATTHEW 6:9)

I once heard about a small group that did a rigorous Bible study on the topic of prayer. Talk about thorough! They scoured God's Word from Genesis through Revelation, reading and dissecting countless scriptural prayers. They looked up all the pertinent Hebrew and Greek words, discussed the wide-ranging thoughts and insights of famous theologians. Their study took months, and during that time, they learned more about prayer than most folks will ever know in a lifetime.

Yet somehow they never actually spent much time praying.

• • •

In the Gospels, we don't find Jesus merely talking about prayer. We see Him praying. The Savior modeled a life of continual communion with the Father.

That's what it means to *pray*. Simply put, prayer is communing with God. It's not a complicated spiritual practice; it's being with the Almighty (and sometimes even talking to Him)! Clement of

Alexandria supposedly described prayer as keeping company with God. That's it. Think of it as drawing close to the one who made you, knows you best, and loves you most . . . and opening your heart.

Prayer typically takes the form of *confession* (seeking forgiveness for wrong thoughts or deeds), *praise* (adoring and enjoying God for who He is), *thanksgiving* (expressing gratitude for divine blessings), *lament* (honestly expressing pain or confusion), *intercession* (lifting up the needs and concerns of others), *petition* or *supplication* (asking God to intervene in your life), and *surrender* (relinquishing control of one's life or situation to God).

• • •

In the Gospels, Jesus prays early in the morning (Mark 1:35) and all through the night (Luke 6:12). Sometimes He's alone in prayer (Matthew 14:23); other times He addresses God in front of large groups (Mark 6:41). We hear Him offer up short petitions (Luke 23:46) and long prayers (John 17), see Him talking to His Father when He is jubilant (Luke 10:21) and also when He is in anguish (Mark 15:34).

Jesus brings His own needs and concerns to the Father (Luke 22:41–44). But mostly He prays for others—His followers (Luke 22:32) and also His enemies (Luke 23:34).

In John 17:20, He even prays for us modern-day believers!

• • •

Prayer, for Jesus, wasn't about *getting things* from the Father, but *being with* the Father. He was, in a certain sense, homesick. When we see how He seemed to ache for time alone with God, it's clear that for Jesus, such moments were snippets of heaven in the midst of a sick and broken world. No wonder He took time—and made time—for prayer.

That's what prayer is: communion with God—opening our heart to Him (even if we don't have much to say when we open our mouth).

Question: In what ways does the prayer life of Jesus challenge your own ideas about, and habits of, prayer?

48

SIN

The refusal or failure to live as God requires

Jesus replied, "Very truly I tell you, everyone who sins is a slave to sin."
(JOHN 8:34)

Suppose we created a world where everyone had access to a top-notch education . . . *and* a good job . . . *and* first-class health-care. And suppose we found cures for all our worst diseases and also managed to solve the hunger, pollution, and clean water crises. And imagine if nuclear proliferation, terrorism, and weather weirdness (droughts, rising temperatures, floods, etc.) came to a screeching halt.

Question: At the mall, would you leave your valuables unattended on a table in the food court, while you went to the restroom?

● ● ●

Sin is such a pervasive and grim reality that the writers of the New Testament used multiple Greek words, with different nuances, to discuss it. The most common word translated *sin*—used by Jesus in the verse above—means "to miss the target."* The word refers to all the ways we fail to be and do what God created us to be and do.

---

* The Greek word *hamartia* means "to miss the target."

Have you always been the absolute best parent or sibling? Are you a flawless friend—perfectly loyal and forgiving and patient, one hundred percent of the time? Were there any moments yesterday in which you could have been kinder or more loving or more generous?

Sin, simply put, is falling short of God's standard of perfect holiness in thought, word, deed, and character. And we're all guilty.

● ● ●

Another New Testament word for sin* (sometimes translated *transgress*) means "to deliberately step across." It refers to intentionally crossing the line between right and wrong. When being quizzed by your spouse, for example, you opt to stop telling the truth and you move into say-anything-in-order-to-save-my-skin mode.

Another word for *sin* means "to slip across."† This isn't premeditated, but it's still wrong and potentially just as damaging. You get angry, let's say, and blurt out some things best left unsaid. You weren't thinking. You weren't careful. You didn't plan any of that, but you're guilty nonetheless.

Still another word conveys the idea of lawlessness.‡ This is overt rebelliousness, living like there are no rules, or like the rules don't apply to yours truly. This is a defiant rejection of God's authority.

● ● ●

The awful news that precedes the gospel's really good news is that we're each guilty of sin (Romans 3:23). Not only that, but as Jesus noted, we're slaves to sin. On our own, we can't stop. When it

---

* The Greek word *parabasis* means "to deliberately step across."
† The verb meaning "to slip across" is *paraptoma* in Greek.
‡ *Anomia* is the New Testament word translated "lawlessness."

comes to falling short, crossing lines, slipping up, and rebelling, we're experts. It's that—sin—that separates us from God (Isaiah 59:2) and lands us on a kind of spiritual death row (Romans 6:23).

The good news is that Jesus came to rescue us (remember, His very name means "the LORD saves"—see Matthew 1:21). By dying the death we deserved (and walking out of the grave), He now lives to offer full pardon to sinners, endless new life to all who will put their trust in Him.

We humans have it within us to fix some of our problems. But only Jesus is the remedy for sin.

49

FREE

To liberate from captivity or oppression

To the Jews who had believed him, Jesus said, "If you hold to my teaching, you are really my disciples. Then you will know the truth, and the truth will set you free." (JOHN 8:31–32)

Four-letter words.
Some make us cringe. Off the top of my head, I think of *work, debt, bill, wait* (plus a few other unmentionables).

But for every foul one, there's another four-letter word that can make us smile . . . words like *love, home, rest,* and *sale* (and don't forget *Wi-Fi*).

Another that's in most people's top ten, the word *free*.

● ● ●

As a verb, *free* means to liberate or deliver from bondage. But how about we dispense with definitions and think in images? Picture Lincoln signing the Emancipation Proclamation. Or middle school kids charging out the school doors on the last day of the year. Or a man walking through prison gates after sixteen plus years of incarceration. Or an AA member tearfully receiving her ten-year sobriety chip.

Being set free means you're no longer at the mercy of whatever previously kept you trapped. There's no feeling quite like freedom. Maybe that's why our language is filled with phrases like free and clear, free spirit, home free, freewheeling, and free as a bird. It's probably why in America the Fourth of July is a party like no other. Freedom calls for serious celebrating and big-time fireworks displays. It says, "No, that hot dog *isn't* so great for you, but if you want it, go for it. Nobody's stopping you."

● ● ●

Worldly freedom is sweet, but the spiritual freedom we experience when we believe the truth of Jesus is staggering.

The good news of Jesus says He came to set us free from both the guilt of sin and the controlling power of it. Faith in Jesus liberates us from all sorts of oppressive things:

- The bogus (but hard-to-shake) idea that we have to somehow earn God's favor (or do certain things to retain it)
- A self-absorbed mindset
- Old hurts that consume us with bitterness
- The frantic compulsion to try to please people
- The stifling need to be perfect
- Wrong attitudes and perspectives and delusional ideas that keep us from flourishing
- Stubborn addictions to sex or food, or ten thousand other things

● ● ●

Long before New Hampshire adopted the saying "Live free or die" as its state motto, the Bible was proclaiming the same truth.

In discussing freedom, Jesus sternly noted, "Everyone who sins is a slave to sin" (John 8:34). Then He added a huge *however*: "If the Son sets you free, you will be free indeed" (John 8:36).

We can trust Christ and experience true, ultimate freedom. Or we can refuse to trust Him and remain at the mercy of sin's destructive power. That's the choice.

To use four-letter words, it's either a life described by words like *hope, wise, true, good, holy,* and *glad.* Or it's one described by words like *grim, fool, sick, pain,* and *dead.*

50

BENT OVER

Twisted instead of straight; deformed rather than whole

And a woman was there who had been crippled by a spirit for eighteen years.
She was bent over and could not straighten up at all. (LUKE 13:11)

Camptocormia—sometimes known as BSS (bent spine syndrome)—is a physical condition, more common among the elderly, in which the lower joints of the spine flex forward, forcing a victim's head and torso to lean over more than forty-five degrees.

Kyphosis (from the Greek word for hump), often labeled *Scheuermann's disease*, describes a condition where the midspine develops a convex curvature, resulting in a severe bowing of the back—forcing the head and face toward the ground.

It seems the evil spirit mentioned in Luke 13:11 used one of these painful, humiliating medical maladies to keep this unnamed woman *bent over*.

Thankfully, Jesus has both the desire and the power to straighten twisted things and people.

• • •

Here we have a real woman in real pain. She's a living parable, a reminder of the Evil One's desire to destroy, and sin's power to debilitate and render us incapable of walking uprightly before the Lord (apart from divine intervention).

• • •

Maybe the miracle preceding THE miracle is that this woman was even present. Consider: She'd been suffering for eighteen *years*! Suppose—out of frustration or bitterness—she had stopped attending synagogue services the previous winter or fourteen years before that, concluding, "Why bother? God doesn't care about me. He's *never* going to answer my prayer!"

Instead, this spiritually stubborn woman kept shuffling to services Sabbath after Sabbath. And on this particular day, Jesus showed up too. Notice that the passage says, "Jesus saw her" (see chapter 40). Think her heart was racing when He "called her over" (Luke 13:12 NLT)?

• • •

Can you imagine this scene? When she gets to where Jesus is, all she can see is the bottom of His robe, His sandaled feet. I picture Christ stooping (see chapter 33), getting down into her very limited field of vision as He speaks liberating words and applies His healing touch.

The incident prompts us to ask ourselves all kinds of questions:

- What exactly is crippling us? Where are our lives "bent over" and locked up?
- Do we put ourselves in situations where we might actually hear Jesus call us? Or more times than not do we avoid him? Run *from* him?
- Are we willing to let Jesus touch us? This isn't a trick question; transformation is tough. It requires readjusting, relearning; it means profound changes in our lives, and it results in new challenges.

- Does the "gospel" we offer to the world set people free or bind them and keep them bound?

Jesus straightens the twisted. If you've got a life like a pretzel (and maybe a crooked past to go with it)—and let's face it, who doesn't?—Jesus is the one you need.

51

SEEK

To pursue or hunt for, to attempt to find

For the Son of Man came to seek and to save the lost. (LUKE 19:10)

Ever stop to consider that all those commuters stuck there with you in rush-hour traffic are seeking various things? Not just alternate routes and interesting podcasts to pass the time, but fortunes, professional help, second opinions—even revenge. Some are swiping left and right in hopes of finding a mate. Most are seeking meaning, enlightenment, or redemption.

What can we say? We are natural-born seekers.

And in our relentless searching, we resemble our Maker.

• • •

Not three pages into the great story of God, everything went to hell (literally). The first humans were living in a paradise so exquisite it would make our prettiest and most exclusive resort look like a landfill by comparison. Yet they rebelled against their Creator and ran away. Inexplicable. Inconceivable. Insane.

The book of Genesis shows God's immediate response wasn't to go off and sulk or go on a smiting spree, but to go searching for His wayward creatures. Ladies and gentlemen, I present to you the two saddest—and simultaneously most hopeful—

verses in the Bible: "Then the man and his wife heard the sound of the Lord God as he was walking in the garden in the cool of the day, and they hid from the Lord God among the trees of the garden. But the Lord God called to the man, 'Where are you?'" (Genesis 3:8–9).

● ● ●

We think of hide-and-seek as a silly kids' game. In actuality it's the story of God's relationship with the human race. We try to hide from God; He makes it His top priority to seek us out.

This is the ministry of Jesus in a nutshell—in His own words, "to seek and to save the lost." How fitting that Jesus made this statement after a comical incident in Jericho. Passing through town, Jesus had noticed the town's top tax official (Zacchaeus, a rich, short, unpopular man) peering down from the leafy boughs of a sycamore tree, and then invited himself to dinner at the man's house!

If that strange story doesn't demonstrate to you the lengths to which the Lord is willing to go to find His beloved creatures, I'm not sure any story ever would.

● ● ●

For people like us, with the bizarre tendency to hide from a God of infinite goodness, the fact of a seeking Savior makes every day better than Christmas. Simon Tugwell expressed it this way: "So long as we imagine it is we who have to look for God, we must often lose heart. But it is the other way about: He is looking for us."

We like to think of ourselves as seekers. The real Seeker, the ultimate Seeker, is Jesus. And there's no place He won't go to find and rescue the ones He loves.

52

SIGN

A supernatural display pointing to the
presence, power, or promise of God

Then some of the Pharisees and teachers of the law said to him,
"Teacher, we want to see a sign from you." (MATTHEW 12:38)

When life spins off in an unexpected direction and God is silent . . . when we're more likely to find Bigfoot in our backyard than faith in our heart, what do we do?

Usually we ask for a *sign*. Even if we don't say the word, it's there, between the lines of our frazzled, frustrated prayers: "Lord, let me know that you *hear me* . . . that you're *here with me*. Please, God. Don't be invisible. Prove that you care. Show me your power. Give me something—a burning bush . . . a wet fleece . . . a still small voice—anything to beat back the doubt."

Signs are reassuring, as well as exciting . . . which is why we're not the first generation to be enamored with them.

● ● ●

In the Bible, the word *sign* typically refers to some kind of supernatural manifestation. *Signs* "signal" or "signify" that God is near and that He is at work. For this reason signs are "significant."

Though biblical signs are almost always wondrous—leaving onlookers awed and amazed—they are never ends in themselves. Jesus didn't perform signs to show off or wow a crowd. He used them for the same reason business owners use commercial signs: to get *attention*, give *information*, and provide *direction*. Signs are never *the* point; rather, they exist *to* point to whatever they're advertising.

Here's an experiment: The next time you're on a trip and hungry, find a fancy restaurant billboard, pull over next to it, and gawk at it. Don't bother following the sign to the actual restaurant two miles up the highway. Just sit there oohing and aahing over the sign itself. See what that does for your growling stomach.

● ● ●

When he wrote his gospel account of the life of Christ, John chose to highlight only a few of Christ's mighty works. Here's his explanation: "Jesus performed many other signs in the presence of his disciples, which are not recorded in this book. But these are written that you may believe that Jesus is the Messiah, the Son of God, and that by believing you may have life in his name" (John 20:30–31).

In other words, if we fixate on the miracles themselves and don't place our faith in the Messiah behind them, the signs have failed to accomplish their purpose.

● ● ●

If a friend were desperately ill, you wouldn't hesitate to ask God for a miracle. And if the Almighty came crashing into the life of an unbelieving family member via "signs and wonders," you wouldn't complain.

The goal is to ask God to work in mighty ways *without* becoming part of the "wicked and adulterous generation" Jesus spoke about. Those are the people who obsess over signs or, worse, *demand* that the Lord do miracles on command (John 4:48; Matthew 16:4). More than signs, we need the Savior. More than proof, we need faith.

Even though it's always nice to see the great works of God with our own eyes, we don't have to see to believe (John 20:29).

53

FISH

Gilled and finned marine creatures that were
a primary food source in the time of Christ—and that
came to symbolize the Christian faith

Jesus said to them, "Bring some of the fish you have just caught."
(JOHN 21:10)

The life of Jesus was extremely fishy.

Professional fishermen made up at least a third of His entourage. (Their decision to switch careers came about when the carpenter-turned-rabbi demonstrated He knew more about fish and fishing than they ever would [see Luke 5:4–11] . . . and after He challenged them to devote their lives to fishing for people instead.)

On at least two occasions, Christ took a few small fish and barley loaves and miraculously treated hungry crowds (numbering in the thousands) to all-you-can-eat feasts (see Mark 6:32–44; 8:1–9). Once, when needing to pay the required temple tax, Jesus told Peter to "go to the lake and throw out your line. Take the first fish you catch; open its mouth and you will find a four-drachma coin. Take it and give it to them for my tax and yours" (Matthew 17:27).

We could keep going. Jesus told fishing stories (Matthew 13:47–50). After His resurrection—to prove He wasn't a phantom—He ate a piece of broiled fish while His slack-jawed followers watched (Luke 24:42). His final miracle—before returning to heaven—involved pointing His fisherman friends to yet another enormous school of fish (John 21:1–13).* After the men dragged their net to shore, Jesus served them a breakfast of roasted fish and bread.

• • •

All this explains why, from the earliest days of the church, the fish has been a symbol of Christianity. The New Testament word translated *fish* is *ichthys*, or—in Greek ἰχθύς. Interestingly, those five Greek letters are the first letters in the words "Jesus Christ, God's Son, Savior."

So when Christians put fish emblems on their cars, it's a way of proclaiming faith in Christ, of saying, "I'm a follower of Jesus." (And—ideally—"Because of that, I don't speed, drive recklessly, or rant at other drivers.")

• • •

What conclusion can we draw from all these gospel references to fish and fishing—besides the obvious fact that Jesus was not a vegetarian? Mostly this: Jesus used fish to illustrate how God meets humanity's deepest needs.

• • •

As metaphors go, "fishing for people" feels, well, awkward. After all, when we fish—using either deception (baits and lures) or force (big, inescapable nets)—the fish that are caught die and are consumed. (What right-thinking fish clamors for *that*?)

Jesus, however, said He came not to kill and destroy, but to give life to the full (John 10:10). Maybe it can help to think

---

* Funny side note: with the resurrected Christ standing there on the beach, one of these fishing fanatics stopped to count the fish in the net! The tally? 153! (See John 21:11.)

of "fishing for people" as snatching people out of death and setting them free in the ocean of God's great love . . . as heaven's eternal catch-and-release program.

54

BREAD

The most basic staple of the human diet from
the earliest times

I am the bread of life. (JOHN 6:48)

Breadless diets (such as Atkins, Paleo, Keto, Whole 30) are all the rage.

For some, this bread boycott is a deliberate effort to avoid gluten, a(n apparently delicious) protein found in grains, which gives dough its elasticity . . . and which causes illness in some people . . . and which also seems to have a magical power that makes most of us gluttons for more bread.

For others, this swearing off of grains is (a) an attempt to avoid carbohydrates—and the blood sugar issues that come with eating lots of high glycemic foods; and/or (b) a way to shed unwanted pounds.

My friends in the no-bread crowd often tell me that, contrary to what I might think, it *is* possible to live without bread. (They usually say this with a faraway look of wistfulness.)

Here is what I can tell you: though it might be possible to steer clear of bread in *your* life, there's no way to avoid it when exploring the life of Christ.

• • •

The Bible's got more bread in it than a Parisian bakery at 6 a.m. Typically the *bread* mentioned in Scripture is literal—primitive loaves made of barley or simple cakes made out of fine flour, then cooked with a bit of oil on griddles, hot rocks, or in ovens.

All the fancier stuff—ciabatta bread, croissants, brioche, and baguettes? You won't find any of that in the Bible. (Though Christian singer Keith Green once joked about the Israelites in the wilderness eating "bamanna bread"; see Exodus 16.)

•   •   •

It's the figurative references to bread in the Bible that should grab our attention. In ancient cultures, people regarded bread (along with water) as vital to existence. Bread was the primary staple in most diets. Without it, people starved to death.

Therefore when Jesus labeled himself "the bread of life" and insisted that people "feed on me" (John 6:57), His point was unmistakable. Christ isn't just nice to have, He's necessary. It's impossible for anyone to live in any kind of meaningful or spiritual way apart from Christ.

Just like your body takes that cinnamon raisin bagel you ate for breakfast and breaks it down into nutrients and minerals that power you through the morning (okay, for about an hour), so when we ingest Christ—when we take Him into our lives hungrily by faith, savoring Him, and letting Him fill us—we find Him powering and sustaining us.

•   •   •

Are you hungry today? Is there a growling, maybe not in your stomach but in your soul? Do you feel spiritually weak or malnourished?

It's time to feast on the one who said, "I am the living bread that came down from heaven. Whoever eats this bread will live forever. This bread is my flesh, which I will give for the life of the world" (John 6:51).

55

GATE

An entryway or passageway

Enter through the narrow gate. For wide is the gate and broad is the road that
leads to destruction, and many enter through it. But small is the gate and
narrow the road that leads to life, and only a few find it. (MATTHEW 7:13–14)

Years ago, I found myself at a massive international airport
(Hartsfield-Jackson in Atlanta) trying to catch a Friday night
flight to the tiny, regional airport 35 miles from my home. I located
the correct concourse and gate number on a bank of monitors listing departures. Then I walked right past concourses A, B, and C,
because what I needed was concourse D.

In concourse D I saw dozens of gates. Convenient ones. Large
ones. Desirable ones, located near good restaurants and restrooms
and cool shops. But I kept walking because none of those gates led
to where I wanted to go.

At the far end of the long concourse, about gate 45, I think
it was (somewhere near the Georgia-Florida line!), I presented
my boarding pass to a weary-looking Delta Airlines agent. She
directed me through a door, down some stairs and out on to the
tarmac. There were jets of all descriptions, in every direction.
But there was only one flight headed for Monroe, Louisiana:
a small puddle jumper, with propellers.* And there was only one

---

* Fitting, since Delta Airlines began in 1925 as a crop-dusting service in Monroe.

doorway through which to enter that plane. When I got on board, I gulped. Only three seats per row, but thankfully plenty of empty seats. Clearly this was not the most in-demand flight out of ATL.

Passing all those gates reminded me of Jesus's words in Matthew 7:13–14.

• • •

In His famous Sermon on the Mount, Jesus talked urgently about two *gates* (the word simply means "entrance" or "passageway"). He described one gate as "wide" and opening to a broad road (picture a big concourse full of shiny, glitzy things). Then He grimly added that this gate "leads to destruction" and that "many enter" it.

Thankfully, He spoke of another gate—one that's narrow and small. According to Jesus, this is the gate we want because it is the only gate that leads to life. And yet, He said, "only a few find it" and step through it. Sobering, huh?

• • •

In another place (John 10:9), Jesus said plainly, "I am the gate." Here is the claim by Jesus that He is not one spiritual option among a bunch of equally valid spiritual options. With this exclusive statement, He was saying, I am the one and only way home (see also John 14:6).

We can believe Jesus and His teaching or we can write Him off as a nutjob or a liar. But, logically, we can't say that His claim is true—along with all the opposing claims of other religions. That's like saying that 2 + 2 = 4 (and also 3, 5—and any other number you want it to be). Either Jesus is the gate to life or He isn't.

• • •

In the great airport of life, we're surrounded by a sea of fellow travelers, many of them choosing gates that have nothing to do with Christ.

Jesus claimed to be the narrow gate that leads to life—the *only* one that does. We have to deal with His statement. We can't ignore it. May God grant us the grace to see the truth and believe it.

56

GET UP

To arise or waken or come to life

Then Jesus said to him, "Get up! Pick up your mat and walk." (JOHN 5:8)

What do you suppose Jesus would say to

- A jobseeker who's down in the dumps (after months of fruitless searching) and doesn't want to get off the couch?
- An apathetic believer who's spiritually catatonic and sleepwalking through life?
- A weary single mom who just wants to pull the covers over her head?
- A widowed ranch owner who feels "lower than a snake's belly"?
- A skeptic whose life—and reasons for *not* believing— are unraveling by the day?

It's presumptuous, if not dangerous, to claim to speak for the Lord. So how about we simply note that throughout the Gospels Jesus commanded assorted people to "Get up!"

• • •

Get up comes from a single Greek verb—*egeiro*—which means to wake up or stir up or arise.

This is the word Jesus used to *rouse* His drowsy disciples in Gethsemane—when they desperately needed to be alert and prayerful (Luke 22:46).

It's the word He spoke to Saul (aka Paul) after blinding the soon-to-be apostle and knocking him off his feet on the Damascus Road. "Get up and ..."—in effect—begin your new life (Acts 9:6).

Egeiro is also the same word Christ used to *resurrect* a dead child (Mark 5:41; Luke 8:54) and a deceased man (Luke 7:14)!

In John 5, Jesus said, "Get up!" to a disabled man who'd been bedridden for almost four decades.

• • •

The effect of this word in the mouth of Christ? Astonishing! The paralyzed man's healing was immediate. Bones strengthened and nerve endings regenerated—instantly. Atrophied muscles suddenly infused with new strength.

And yet the man would never have known any of this miraculous power apart from taking Jesus at His word, lifting his torso, and attempting to stand. He had to trust that with Christ's command came a new capacity to carry out the command. In short, the guy who had been a stranger to exercise for thirty-eight years had to exercise *faith*.

Can't you see him in your mind's eye? Beaming, laughing, leaping like a deer (Isaiah 35:6) as he gathered up his mat and ran off to show people his new legs?

• • •

Maybe you're realizing you could stand to be more alert or more alive. Or maybe you've been knocked down (or beaten down) for some time now, and though it's no fun to be down in the dumps, you've gotten used to it. You're comfortably miserable.

What if Jesus is telling you right now to "Get up!"? And what if you took the Lord at His word?

Come awake! Come to life! Refuse to stay down! Trust Christ and get up!

57

HELL

The place where unrepentant sinners experience
eternal separation from God

You snakes! You brood of vipers! How will you escape being
condemned to hell? (MATTHEW 23:33)

Hell.
Surely if Christians were to pick the one biblical teaching
that causes them to squirm most, it would be this one. The very
idea of hell is sickening, the thought too terrible for words. And
yet . . .

The Gospels show the Lord talking frequently and matter-of-
factly about *hell*. He describes it as a place of eternal fire (Matthew
5:22; 18:9; Mark 9:43)—twice calling it a "blazing furnace" in
Matthew 13.

If we take Jesus at His word, hell is a place of darkness, weeping, and gnashing of teeth (Matthew 8:12).

• • •

The Greek word most often translated *hell* in the New Testament
is *gehenna*, which also happened to be the name of a deep, narrow
ravine on the southern outskirts of Jerusalem.

In Old Testament times this valley was a notorious site where
certain Israelite kings made sacrifices to false gods, some even
burning their children alive in pagan rituals (2 Kings 16:3)! Con-

trary to what many of us have heard (and believed), there's no hard evidence this valley had become a smoldering, smoky garbage dump by the time of Christ. Nevertheless, because of its grim history, this ravine serves as a vivid picture of where a life of corruption and degradation leads. Among the Jews, Gehenna was universally associated with wicked things and evil people.

• • •

In recent times, some Christians have wondered if perhaps the biblical descriptions of hell's fire are meant to be taken in a figurative way—similar, say, to the verses that speak metaphorically of God's "wings."

Here's what we can say for sure. Whether or not Jesus *was* warning of literal fire, it isn't flames that will make hell hellish. The real anguish of hell can be seen in the first three words of this statement of Christ: "Depart from me, you who are cursed, into the eternal fire prepared for the devil and his angels" (Matthew 25:41).

"Depart from me." *There* is the unspeakable horror of hell. Separation from Jesus *forever.* Endless alienation from the one true God who is pure goodness and the source of all good things.

• • •

When you think about it, hell is entirely logical. Why would people who want nothing to do with God during their brief time on earth want to be with God for all eternity? C. S. Lewis was right when he said that we could think of hell as God essentially saying to hard-hearted, unrepentant people, "All right, then, have it your way."*

---

* C. S. Lewis, *The Great Divorce* (New York: Collier Books/MacMillan Publishing Company, 1946), 72–73.

This grim thought is all the more reason for believers to do two things: (1) Ask God to move powerfully in the lives of their friends and loved ones who are far from God, and (2) live in such a way that those folks see how beautiful it is to walk closely with Christ.

58

HEAVEN

The dwelling place of God, his angels, and his people

For I have come down from heaven not to do my will but to do
the will of him who sent me. (JOHN 6:38)

What happens after death?

Even if people don't ask this question out loud, everyone wrestles with some version of it.

It's definitely worth pondering. When, as the Good Book puts it, we "go the way of all the earth" (1 Kings 2:2) and "breathe our last" (Genesis 35:29), what's next? Nothingness? Or some kind of existence beyond this life?

Is there a place called *heaven*?

• • •

The word *heaven* is used in two primary ways in the Bible: (1) to refer to what we would call the sky above or even outer space*; and, more importantly, (2) to speak of the dwelling place of the triune God (1 Kings 8:30; Jonah 1:9; Matthew 6:9) and those associated

---

* The ancient Hebrews thought the sky was contained within a giant transparent dome that encircled the earth. Outside that dome were waters that gave the sky its blue color. Beyond the waters was heaven above, where God dwells.

with Him (angelic beings and redeemed people—see Nehemiah 9:6; Mark 13:32).

While He didn't say a lot about heaven,* Jesus did make several intriguing comments about it. In the gospel of John He claimed, "I have come down from heaven" (John 6:38). Later, He talked about "My Father's house" (John 14:1–4), describing an actual place with "many rooms." He spoke of going there to prepare a place for His followers, adding that He would "come back and take you to be with me."

Numerous times in the gospel of John, Jesus spoke to His followers of *eternal life*, which He defined as knowing God—intimately and personally—through faith in Him (John 17:3; see also 14:6).

Put all that together, and we could say that in John's gospel Jesus describes heaven as an actual place in which we get to experience the actual presence of God.

• • •

Late in his life, the apostle John was given a stunning glimpse of Christ in His future glory (we know this series of visions as the book of Revelation†). This final book of the Bible is remarkable in that it describes not an ethereal heavenly realm, but a "new heaven and a new earth" (Revelation 21:1). The preview it gives suggests a kind of marriage, a beautiful coming together of spiritual and physical realities—except that all of it will be new. Resurrected, fully redeemed Christians living with the triune God (v. 3) in a fully restored world.

To hear John tell it, just as Jesus came down to earth in history to seek and save sinners, so one day in the future heaven will also come down. Eternity will consist of the best of both worlds.

---

* Mostly Jesus referred to heaven with reference to the kingdom ("the kingdom of heaven" or "kingdom of God") and also the place where God lives.
† For the record it's "Revelation" (singular), not "Revelations" (plural).

• • •

The clear teaching of Jesus is that this life is not the end; rather, it's the end of the beginning. The eternal life that begins for us here on earth when we enter into a relationship with God through faith in Christ (John 17:3) will continue beyond this world. Except that there (and then) our experience of Him won't be tainted by the fall or by our flesh . . . or veiled by imperfect faith. Our minds will be fully renewed. We'll be like Him (1 John 3:2).

Best of all, we will see His face (Revelation 22:4).

59

CHURCH

An assembly of the Lord's people,
called out from the world
to live for Him in the world

And I tell you that you are Peter, and on this rock
I will build my church, and the gates of Hades
will not overcome it. (MATTHEW 16:18)

For some people the word *church* triggers thoughts of candles and choirs, pews and stained glass windows. For others it means guitar music and upraised arms in a storefront or a building that resembles a mall.

Some describe church as "my lifeline," "my family of faith," or "the place I found peace and purpose." Others, tragically, describe their church experience with haunting phrases like "a bunch of finger-pointing hypocrites" or "where I walked *away* from the faith."

What in the world did Jesus have in mind when He thought up the idea of church?

• • •

To be fair, Jesus didn't say much about church.* The word is found on His lips just three times in the four gospels. This means we have to ferret out our information about how churches are supposed to function through the *descriptions* found in the book of Acts and the *prescriptions* found in the New Testament epistles.

The word *church* literally means "the called-out ones." In the New Testament, *church* refers to local assemblies (or gatherings) of followers of Jesus (Acts 14:23; Romans 16:5; 1 Corinthians 1:2). *Church* also designates all believers in Christ, in every location and generation (Ephesians 1:22).

• • •

It's common to think of church as a building where we attend weekend meetings in order to sing, pray, and listen to someone talk about the Bible. It's also wrong.

Church isn't a facility or a religious event. It's a spiritual family. The church is people (1 Corinthians 16:19) . . . people who once shared a common *problem* (separation from God because of sin) and a common *need* (forgiveness and new life), and who now—because of faith in Christ—share a common *hope* (salvation!) and a common *mission* (helping others experience new life in Christ).

Peter, who helped launch the church only a few weeks after Christ's resurrection, described believers in this intriguing way: "living stones . . . being built into a spiritual house" (1 Peter 2:5).

• • •

---

* Only that (a) He would build it—and not even hell itself would stop Him or it (Matthew 16:18); and (b) it's the gathering of saints meant to help each other turn from sin and make it safely home (Matthew 18:15–17).

Because the church is people—a bunch of flawed, still-under-construction saints (Philippians 1:6), it's a mixed bag. In the spring, your church experience might be exhilarating. By the fall, you may feel nothing but exasperation.

Go be part of a local church body anyway. Your soul needs it (and all those other souls need what only you can add).

Show up. Sing out. Look around. Plug in.

Make an effort to get to know others in the flock. Join a small group. Then use the gifts and resources God has given you to serve both believers and those we could call "pre-believers."

The old comparison between the church and Noah's ark is true. Inside things can sometimes get pretty stinky. But that's nothing compared to the storm on the outside.

60

FORGIVEN

To be pardoned or released from the guilt of wrongdoing

Then Jesus said to her, "Your sins are forgiven." (LUKE 7:48)

Rounding the corner, you catch the faint hint of an old, familiar smell. Instantly—without even trying—your memory is triggered. You find yourself transported to that stupid place, that shameful moment you'd erase from your past, if only you could. Your knees go weak. Your stomach knots up with regret.

You round the aisle in the grocery store and there she is. (Thank God she was looking at the avocados, and not in your direction!) You quickly turn your cart 180 degrees and dart down the cereal aisle, and as you do, you find your heart racing, a sharp anger rising within you. The outrageous things that woman did and said. The unfair way she made *you* out to be the villain for the bad situation *she* caused.

The word from the Word for such situations?
Forgiven.

• • •

The Greek word we translate into English as *forgive* communicated the idea of hurling or sending off. In legal settings it was used to convey the idea of releasing (from a debt or from guilt). Thus, in biblical usage, a person who is *forgiven* has been pardoned from wrongdoing.

Thus the beauty and power in passages that speak of God hurling our iniquities (our sins) into the depths of the sea (Micah 7:19) ... or Israel's high priest symbolically laying the sins of Israel on the head of a scapegoat and sending it off into the wilderness (Leviticus 16:21–22) ... or Jesus telling a story about a benevolent master canceling the huge debt of one of his servants—then being angered when he discovered that same servant was unwilling to cancel the much smaller debt of one of his fellow servants (Matthew 18:21–35).

• • •

"Forgive and forget" is a phrase that gets tossed around a lot in church world. Here's what that doesn't mean: Forgiveness isn't forgetting in the sense of erasing memories from your brain. Our all-knowing God doesn't do that—He doesn't get amnesia or dementia. In fact, His eternal Word contains detailed stories of the glaring sins of certain saints!

God forgets our sins in this sense: He doesn't keep bringing them up. He doesn't shame us or condemn us. He's well aware of all our failures (otherwise He couldn't be all-knowing). But because of the forgiveness of Jesus, He doesn't hold those things against us.

• • •

If you've trusted in Jesus to forgive you, but you're still hearing condemning whispers, understand this: That's not the voice of God talking to you. Spend some time meditating on Micah 7:19 or Luke 7:36–50.

If you've trusted in Jesus to forgive you, but you're still getting worked up over the wrongs someone has done to you, ask God for the grace to forgive your debtors as He has forgiven your debts (Matthew 6:12). Refuse to be petty. Let go of your grudges and resentments.

In the kingdom of Jesus, forgiven people are forgiving people.

61

TOUCH

To make contact with another

Jesus reached out his hand and touched the man. "I am willing," he said. "Be clean!" And immediately the leprosy left him. (LUKE 5:13)

Think touch is no big deal? Then why do we go around saying things like "Stay in touch" or "He's lost touch with reality" or "That speech was so touching"?

And how do we explain all those poor Romanian children back in the 1980s who were tragically warehoused in understaffed orphanages, never hugged or held . . . and who developed severe attachment disorders, delayed cognitive development, and a host of other medical and emotional problems?

And what do we make of the 2010 study conducted by Dacher Keltner, a social psychologist at UC Berkeley, that showed a correlation between NBA teams that engage in more high fives, chest bumps, hugs, back pats, butt slaps, etc.—and *winning*?

There's a reason Jesus was a master toucher (not just a master teacher).

● ● ●

The most common word translated *touch* in the New Testament is the Greek *hapto.* It typically means "to make physical contact, to grasp firmly," or even "to hold on to."

Reading the Gospels we see Jesus indiscriminately touching all sorts of people and things. He held babies and children with tenderness and joy (Luke 18:15). He touched and restored the sick (Matthew 8:15); gently patted terrified disciples (Matthew 17:7); and placed His fingers on the eyes of the blind (Matthew 9:29; 20:34), the ears of the deaf (Mark 7:33), and on the *severed* ear of one of His enemies (Luke 22:51).

More shocking is the fact that Jesus was indifferent to certain Jewish prohibitions against touching. Instead of steering clear of things that would render Him "unclean," Jesus drew closer. With compassion, He touched "untouchable" lepers (Matthew 8:3); with power, He grasped those who were dead (Luke 7:14; 8:53–54) and pulled them back to life.

It didn't take long for word to get out that Christ's touch was utterly transforming. Consequently, everywhere He went, sick people and sinners reached out in hopes of touching Him first (Matthew 9:20; 14:36; Mark 5:27–31; 6:56; Luke 8:44–47).

• • •

Science is now discovering the truth that Jesus modeled two millennia ago: Compassionate, loving touches have a healing effect—both physically and emotionally. Studies show that appropriate touch triggers the release of oxytocin, which has a soothing and bonding effect, and helps combat stress.

• • •

We live in an era when touching is often considered taboo. It's important to be oh-so-careful. However, appropriate, heartfelt, God-honoring, people-blessing touching has never been more needed. As members of the body of Christ, it's up to us to touch others with His love . . . in every appropriate way.

62

SERVE

To wait upon and meet needs

For even the Son of Man did not come to be served, but to serve,
and to give his life as a ransom for many. (MARK 10:45)

In the opening sentence of his gospel, Mark lays all his cards on the table. He calls Jesus the Christ (the long-awaited Jewish Messiah). To bolster his case, for the next eight chapters Mark shows Jesus preaching, gathering disciples, angering the Jewish religious leaders, and performing assorted miracles.

All this is followed by a pivotal scene in the middle of the book in which Jesus bluntly asks His followers, essentially, "What do you have to say about me now?" Peter, replies, in effect, "I say that you are the Christ" (Mark 8:27–30).

Peter utters the C-word. He speaks the title that makes Jewish hearts race. All those messianic expectations . . . all those mental images of a powerful king like David sweeping in and humiliating Israel's enemies and leading the nation to national glory. This was the stuff of the best daydreams!

So imagine the disciples' shock when Jesus immediately begins talking about His imminent suffering and death (8:31; 9:31). Or when He says, shortly after that, that He came, not to be served but to serve, and to give His life as a ransom (10:45).

• • •

"Hi, I'm Kelsie," the smiling waitress says. "I'll be your server tonight. I'll be taking care of you."

Believe it or not, this is precisely what the word *serve* meant in the first century. To serve was, literally, to "wait on a table; to provide; to take care of" (Luke 10:40; John 12:2). Serving—being a servant—was not a dignified position. It was a place of humility (much like it is now). A servant existed solely to meet the needs of another.

And thus the stunning statement of Jesus—the Christ, the anointed Son of God, heaven's King—that He came not to be served. Rather, "I am among you as one who serves" (Luke 22:27).

• • •

Sure enough, in the final chapters of his gospel, Mark shows Jesus shattering every Jewish expectation of Messiah. He rides into Jerusalem not on a war horse but on a humble donkey. He receives a crown all right, but it's a crown of thorns—meant as a cruel joke. Rather than ascend to a throne, He's raised up on a cross. Ironically, the only person who confidently declares that the limp ragdoll of a man suspended there between heaven and earth is the Christ, the Son of God, is a Roman centurion (Mark 15:39).

• • •

Take a few moments to slowly and carefully read John 13:1–17. (This is the famous scene the night before His crucifixion, in which Jesus washes the feet of His disciples.)

But don't simply read the passage. Put yourself in that upper room with Christ and the twelve disciples. Imagine, Jesus, stripped down like a lowly servant, crouching at your feet with a bucket of water. Picture Him looking up at you. Try to see Him in your mind's eye, taking off your old, smelly shoes and wiping away the dirt from between your toes and off your ankles.

This is the eternal King of heaven. What do you think and feel now?

63

FULFILL

To cause to happen, to finish, to bring to completion

This took place to fulfill what was spoken through the prophet.
(MATTHEW 21:4)

At their fiftieth-anniversary extravaganza, the family matriarch squeezes the hand of her soul mate. Long ago she dreamed every bit of this: Launching out on an adventure with her sweetheart, building a life together, having a big house full of kids (and one day, grandkids), leaving a rich legacy.

While one of her sons does a (pretty terrible) karaoke version of "Celebration," his crazy brother, tie wrapped around his head like a bandanna, tries (in vain) to breakdance. The grandkids and their spouses are all ROTFL.

Watching this boisterous, still-growing brood evokes a flood of memories: More blessings than she can count. Some rough patches she'd just as soon forget. God's faithfulness every step of the way.

She scans the room, and everything gets blurry. Dabbing at her eyes, she smiles, leans against her beloved husband, and whispers, "My heart is full."

• • •

There's a word that's found multiple times in the Gospels that conveys this idea of being full or complete. It's the Greek word *plēroō* (don't worry—that won't be on the test). Dozens of times Jesus is described as saying this or accomplishing that in order "to fulfill" the Scripture.

What's the meaning? Simply this: Centuries before, the Jewish prophets—in predicting the coming of Israel's Messiah—had set forth a number of indicators that would mark a certain individual as the Christ, the combination Savior-King promised by God.

With this word *fulfill*, the gospel writers repeatedly claimed that Jesus checked all the boxes and satisfied all the requirements and expectations of Messiah. And, as such, He alone can turn our deepest longings into vivid realities.

● ● ●

People go back on their word all the time and for all sorts of reasons. Sometimes a plan is poorly thought through or just too grandiose. Sometimes a pledge-maker is incompetent and full of hot air— or worse, a scammer. The reasons are irrelevant. The fact is, whenever dreams go unrealized, hope dwindles. And when promises are unkept, faith fizzles.

This is why it's so significant that Jesus *fulfilled* more than a hundred Old Testament prophecies about the Messiah. He carried out all God's intentions. He brought the Almighty's epic plan to completion.

No wonder He yelled triumphantly at the very end of His life, "It is finished!" (John 19:30).

● ● ●

Jesus has fulfilled all God's high expectations *of* us, and He's in the process of making good on all God's wonderful promises *to* us. The only question is, Will we let the fulfillment He offers be *in* us?

Don't you want to be able to say, "My heart is full" (and not just at your fiftieth-wedding-anniversary wingding)?

Ask Christ to fill and complete you in this very moment.

64

TRANSFIGURED

To transform or change in form

After six days Jesus took Peter, James and John with him
and led them up a high mountain, where they were all alone.
There he was transfigured before them. (MARK 9:2)

Of all the *Wow!* stories the Gospels tell about Jesus, this is one
of the *wow*iest.

Jesus took Peter, James, and John, the three disciples closest to
Him—His inner circle, if you will—up "a high mountain." Mount
Tabor, perhaps? Mount Carmel? Mount Hermon? The gospel
writers don't say *where.* They only describe—or *try* to describe—
what happened there.

On an unnamed mountain, the three ex-fishermen saw and
heard spectacular things.

Jesus was *transfigured* right before their eyes.

• • •

The Greek word translated *transfigured* is where we get our
English word *metamorphosis.* It means "to be changed or
transformed."

Mark described the scene this way: "[Jesus's] clothes became dazzling white, whiter than anyone in the world could bleach them" (9:3). Matthew said His garments were "as white as light" (17:2). Luke described them "as bright as a flash of lightning" (9:29). In other words, they were shining, gleaming. Matthew added that it wasn't just the Lord's clothing that was radiant. "His face shone like the sun" (17:2).

That's not all. While Jesus was in this glorious state, two heroes of the Jewish faith—Moses and Elijah—suddenly appeared and engaged Christ in conversation (Luke 9:30–31).

Matthew, doing his best Captain Obvious impersonation, wrote that the three disciples "fell facedown to the ground, terrified" (17:6).

Most people lose the ability to speak when they become frightened. But some—Peter was one—start babbling nervously, not even realizing what they're saying (Luke 9:33).

As Peter was yammering on, a cloud formed and enveloped them, and a heavenly voice—the voice of the Almighty—quickly shushed Peter.

Then as suddenly as the experience began, it ended. Everything went back to normal again (or as normal as life ever gets when Jesus is around).

• • •

A German theologian by the name of Rudolf Otto (1869–1937) wrote extensively about *numinous* experiences. The word comes from the Latin word *numen*, which refers to a sense of the divine presence. Otto called such encounters the "mysterium tremendum," because, he argued, unlike "ordinary" moments in life, they prompt a deep sense of mystery and awe and holy fear.

Could any experience ever be more numinous than the transfiguration? For a few moments, the three disciples were allowed to see beyond the (perfect) humanity of Jesus. They witnessed the glorious majesty of His divine nature.

• • •

Writing to Christians years later, the apostle Peter referenced his brief, numinous glimpse of Christ at the transfiguration. In so many words he said, "The whole world will get to see that unveiled glory when Jesus comes again" (2 Peter 1:16–18).

Imagine that … watching the radiant, transfigured one transfigure (or transform) the entire universe!

65

LISTEN

To pay careful attention in order to perceive
and take to heart

A voice came from the cloud, saying, "This is my Son, whom I have
chosen; listen to him." (LUKE 9:35)

Assuming (a) you don't have some sort of auditory impairment; and (b) you're not walking around wearing noise-canceling headphones, you hear various sounds all day, every day.

What can you hear *as you read this sentence*? The tick of a clock? Your stomach growling? Classic rock music coming from the neighbor's backyard? Maybe you hear the sound of muffled voices in the next room or the rumble of a truck on a nearby street.

Let's face it: Hearing doesn't take great effort—or really any effort at all. When our ears are in good working condition, hearing is automatic. We can do it with our eyes closed, with both hands tied behind our backs!

It's when we decide to pause and pay close attention to exactly *what* we're hearing (and what it might mean) that we engage in the rarer, more intentional, more important art of *listening*.

● ● ●

A single Greek verb gets translated both *hear* and *listen* in the Gospels. Occasionally it refers simply to the physiological ability to detect sounds and noises (Matthew 11:5; Mark 7:37). More often the word has a bigger and broader meaning: "to pay attention" or "to respond to, to understand," or even "to obey."

Interesting that when the Son's glory was revealed to His three closest disciples—at the transfiguration—the heavenly command was "listen to him."

• • •

Ever tried to listen to two or more things at once? (Dumb question, right?) The kids are arguing, let's say, *and* your spouse is talking to you, *and* the voice on TV is saying something you wanted to catch. Or how about back in the day on road trips when your car's AM/FM radio would start picking up two different stations at once? Neither a pleasant nor profitable experience.

To really *listen* to someone we have to make a conscious, willful choice to turn off (or tune out) all other sounds. *Listening* requires our full attention.

• • •

The 2001 film *A Beautiful Mind* tells the inspiring story of John Nash, a Nobel Prize–winning economist and mathematician, who suffered from schizophrenia. In a scene near the end, Nash says softly, "We all hear voices; we just have to decide which ones we're going to listen to."

That's it. Hearing might be automatic, but listening is a choice. God tells us the voice of Jesus is the one most worthy of our attention—which explains why Jesus often said, "If any man has ears to hear, let him hear."

The idea in this biblical emphasis on listening and hearing is simple: Focus! Pay attention! Because if we don't, we'll lead superficial, distracted lives. Today, amid the chorus of voices that surrounds you, lock in on the voice of Christ.

66

WEPT

To have shed tears

Jesus wept. (JOHN 11:35)

God might have created us in such a way that whenever we get sad,* our ears would start wiggling or our fingernails would turn blue. He didn't. He made us so that our eyes fill with salty fluid.

If we don't stifle such emotions, that salty liquid spills out and rolls down our cheeks. When we really get going (give in to what some people call "ugly crying"), our whole bodies shake, our vision blurs, our eyes get puffy and red—oh, and our noses start running too. When we finally pull it together, we often have a headache as a souvenir of the occasion.

No need to feel embarrassed—even if you're a masculine, male, manly guy who's "not supposed to cry." Jesus was "a man of sorrows and acquainted with grief" (Isaiah 53:3 ESV). He shed His share of tears.

• • •

What a scene . . . Can you see it in your mind? Jesus is standing at the tomb of His friend Lazarus, watching the dead man's sisters,

---

* We can also cry from joy or frustration or fear.

Mary and Martha, mourn . . . and He suddenly loses it. The Savior breaks down. "Jesus wept" is how the eyewitness John put it.

Can you see Him there, tears running down into His beard? If He is who He says He is, then this is God Almighty come to earth . . . all choked up and broken up. This is the all-powerful Creator . . . crying.

Luke, in his gospel, wrote about another tear-filled occasion. "As [Jesus] approached Jerusalem and saw the city, he wept over it" (Luke 19:41). In this case, Jesus was saddened over the nation's refusal to accept Him as its rightful King and Savior. Luke used a different word for *wept*, one that conveys the idea of deep sorrow and mourning, in this case, over the fact of coming judgment.

• • •

Why? Why would Jesus cry at Lazarus's tomb (especially when He already had plans to raise His friend from the dead)? Probably He wept at the brokenness of the world. He never meant for it to include things like cemeteries and caskets. Certainly He cried out of empathy for His friends.

Empathetic people are like tuning forks. Put two tuning forks of the same pitch near each other, and strike one of them. After a couple seconds, if you silence its vibration with your hand, the second fork will continue sounding the original tone, even though it was never struck!

That's empathy. Resonating with the pain of another. Sharing his hurt. Or letting her tears bring you to tears. Nobody ever did or ever will empathize better than Jesus.

• • •

When's the last time you bawled your eyes out?

Or if you can't remember back that far, what things in life tend to get you choked up or misty-eyed?

Here's what we know: The Lord weeps with His weeping friends. And maybe the reason He collects our tears in a bottle (see Psalm 56:8 NLT) is because in the world to come, He plans to pour them out into an ocean of infinite joy. Maybe for every drop of grief we experience in this life, He plans to give us twenty thousand leagues of gladness in the world to come.

67

TRULY

An adverb—and one of Christ's favorite words—
that implies firmness, reliability, and authority

Jesus answered, "Very truly I tell you, no one can enter the kingdom of
God unless they are born of water and the Spirit." (JOHN 3:5)

It's a word Jesus said almost as frequently as millennials say "like," or people on TV say "at the end of the day."

Truly. (Or, as it's translated in the old Authorized King James Version, *verily.*)

What a meaningful and powerful word!

•   •   •

Truly is the English translation of the ancient Hebrew word *amen,* which actually means firm or faithful. It's a solemn, strong affirmation. It conveys the idea of "For sure!" or "Indeed!" or "Absolutely!" The word *truly* suggests certainty, provides assurance, and is meant to inspire confidence (and obedience). Inherent in it is the idea, "Here's something you can take to the bank," or "You can bet your life on this." Or, as country folk like to say, "This is how the cow ate the cabbage."

Around *one hundred times* in the Gospels Jesus prefaced His comments to individuals or crowds by declaring, "Truly, I say to you . . ." The obvious implication? "Perk up. Pay attention. I'm not just chewing the fat or shooting the breeze here. I'm downloading eternal Truth. I'm giving you authoritative realities that you can (and should!) stake your life on and build your life upon."

Sometimes, for effect—when an audience really, REALLY needed to grasp a certain truth—Jesus used the word *truly* twice in a row.* Whenever we see a *truly* or a *double truly* . . . a holy alarm should sound in our hearts.

• • •

Saying "Amen" at the end of a prayer—or following an excellent statement in a sermon—is like saying, "So be it!" or "Yes, let it be!" or "I agree!" It's a way of affirming what has just been spoken.

When Jesus says "amen" (*truly*) as He begins to speak or teach, He's saying, "Regardless of what you might feel or what the world is telling you, this is the way it is." His words are not only reliable, but also authoritative. No wonder in Revelation 3:14, Jesus is revealed as "the Amen, the faithful and true witness."

• • •

I personally think a national ban on the word *like* and the phrase *at the end of the day* would be a welcome thing. A moratorium on the word *truly*? Never.

In a world where falsehoods flourish and where almost nothing is sure, do we need this word of Jesus more than ever?

Truly we do!

---

* In John's gospel, Jesus says this word twice in a row ("Truly, truly, I say to you") on twenty-five different occasions!

68

WHOEVER

Any person, without restriction

For God so loved the world that he gave his one and only Son, that whoever believes in him shall not perish but have eternal life. (JOHN 3:16)

One of the loudest and most frequent criticisms against Christianity is that it is *exclusive*.

If you've been a follower of Christ for any length of time at all, you've probably heard someone say (maybe even say *to you*), "Where do you Christians get off claiming Jesus is the only way to God? What about people who devoutly practice other religions? Do you really think you're better? How can you be so narrow-minded? Why would you embrace a faith that is so intolerant?"

These sorts of questions would be problematic, except for the fact that Jesus used one extremely inclusive word again and again and again.

That word is *whoever*.

•　•　•

The word *whoever* means "anybody and everybody, without restriction." (Does that sound exclusive to you?) *Whoever* is an open, nondiscriminatory invitation. It says all are eligible, all are welcome—Muslims, Buddhists, atheists, CINOs (Christians in name only), anyone. Look at just three of the ways Jesus used it:

- "Whoever hears my word and believes him who sent me has eternal life and will not be judged but has crossed over from death to life" (John 5:24).
- "Whoever acknowledges me before others, I will also acknowledge before my Father in heaven" (Matthew 10:32).
- "Whoever loses their life for my sake will find it" (Matthew 10:39).

In spite of reports to the contrary, the Bible assures us that God doesn't play favorites (Acts 10:34; Romans 2:11). And Jesus, by repeatedly using the word *whoever,* made it clear that anyone, anywhere can be saved. Not by jumping through religious hoops, but by trusting in Him.

• • •

As to the common criticisms cited above, the reason Christians claim Jesus is the only way to God is because that's what He claimed (John 14:6). Repeating His words isn't bragging or gloating—as if any person anywhere has anything to brag or gloat about. It's simply stating what Christ himself said.

Maybe, instead of fuming and fussing over how many ways there are to God, we should be rejoicing that there is at least one way. It's true that Jesus said the "road that leads to life" is narrow and "only a few find it" (Matthew 7:14); however, that doesn't change the fact that whoever desires to get on the road to life can access it. Jesus is an equal-opportunity Savior. He responds to all who call on Him.

• • •

Spend some time today thinking about the astonishing grace that flows from the pronoun *whoever.* This three-syllable word warmly embraces liars and cheats, those with great fame or great shame, deadbeat dads and mass murderers. Are you an addict, a felon, a big religious fake? Good news! *Whoever* includes you.

Welcome this word of ultimate welcome. Even better, accept the one who used it so indiscriminately.

Then let *whoever* alter the way you interact with whomever you meet today.

69

GIVE

To bestow something to someone;
to present a gift to another

... remembering the words the Lord Jesus himself said: "It is more
blessed to give than to receive." (ACTS 20:35)

From the womb to the tomb, all Jesus did was *give*.

While still in utero, He gave His astonished mom and adoptive dad plenty to ponder (Matthew 1:18–22; Luke 1:29–34; 2:19). As a child, He routinely gave them scares (Matthew 2:13; Luke 2:41–50)—and, no doubt, a few gray hairs.

When He grew up, He gave some restless young men the invitation of a lifetime (Mark 1:15–17). When they said yes to His outlandish offer, He gave them orders (Matthew 8:18), authority (Matthew 10:1; 28:18), and experiences neither they nor the world would ever forget (John 21:25).

Jesus spent His waking hours giving God glory (John 8:29), sinners grace (Luke 19:1–10), religious hypocrites fits (Matthew 23), halfhearted followers pause (Luke 9:57–62).

We could go on and on listing the things Jesus gave ... rest to the weary (Matthew 11:28), food to the hungry (Mark 6:33–44; 8:1–13), health to the sick (Mark 1:32–34), freedom to those in bondage (Luke 4:18).

Leave it to the ultimate Giver to also be the ultimate Gift (John 3:16).

• • •

We ooh and ahh over certain Bible words because they contain cool nuances that aren't always obvious at first glance. For example, Paul's command in 1 Timothy 4:7 to "train" yourself (to be godly) is where we get our word "gymnasium."

The word *give* isn't like that. It means just what we think: to bestow, to hand over something to another. Whatever we truly *give* is a gift.

Jesus shows us that God is the consummate Giver. He's not a dealmaker. (Salvation doesn't come with conditions.) Nor is God in the loan business. (Loans have to be paid back.) God gives. No strings attached.

• • •

Jesus—God's living, breathing Gift to the world—gave His followers this nugget, "It's more blessed to give than to receive" (Acts 20:35). (If anyone would know about this topic, it would be Him.) The idea is that when we grasp how extravagantly and faithfully the Lord gives to us, we are freed up to become generous givers ourselves (Luke 6:38). We don't have to go through life clutching at, much less hoarding, earthly things. We don't have to be stingy with our time or parcel out love like we only have enough to last until tomorrow night.

"Freely you have received; freely give" (Matthew 10:8), the Giver said. This is Jesus-speak for "You can never out-give me."

• • •

Maybe you're at a place where you feel you have nothing to give. That's okay. No need to panic. Lift your face, your empty soul to heaven. Let the Lord give you himself—and anything else you need.

Open your hands. Open your heart. And when He fills them, keep them open. Instead of clutching and grasping, find the greater blessing that comes from being a blessing—not just being blessed.

70

REMAIN

To stay, dwell, or live in a certain place

Remain in me, as I also remain in you. No branch can bear fruit by itself; it must
remain in the vine. Neither can you bear fruit unless you remain in me.

(JOHN 15:4)

I f you knew you were dying tomorrow, but got the chance to
eat a final meal with your loved ones tonight . . . what sorts
of things would you talk about?

I'm guessing you wouldn't waste your waning moments
on small talk. Rather than idle chitchat, you'd bring up important
matters. You'd steer the conversation oh so carefully, knowing
that last words are, as the old saying goes, lasting words.

This is, of course, what Jesus did on the night before His death.
He spent His last few hours reminding His followers of the things
that matter most. And one of His most urgent commands was,
"*Remain* in me" (John 15:4; emphasis added).

● ● ●

The Greek word rendered "remain" means "to stay in a place."
In older versions of the Bible, it gets translated "abide." We don't
say *abide* very often, if ever. It sounds old-fashioned. But perhaps
you've visited a friend or relative who greeted you at the front door
with the phrase, "Welcome to our humble abode!" An abode is
a dwelling, a house, a place you live in. It's where you *abide*.

That's the timeless idea Jesus was communicating to His followers on His final night: "I want you to make your home here, *with* me, *in* me. I don't want us to just be neighbors who occasionally wave to each other across the cul-de-sac. I don't want you merely spending a few nights and then moving on. I want you to move in."

• • •

Strong attachment, deep connection, intimacy—those are the ideas in the command to *remain*. To illustrate this, Jesus used an agricultural image we can appreciate even if we've never set foot inside a vineyard. At harvest time, expect to find the intact branches on a healthy grapevine loaded with clusters of grapes. And on those grape branches that have been snapped or partially severed? Nothing. (At least nothing worth eating.)

• • •

In our culture, everything feels temporary. Nothing seems like it *remains*. After thirty years, the quiet, dutiful husband up and leaves his stunned wife. The beloved old bistro up the street suddenly shuts its doors. The star player bolts to a new team for bigger bucks. (Fans should feel lucky the entire team didn't move away to a bigger city.)

This is the restless era in which we find ourselves. The thought of remaining sometimes feels like an anchor, like it's keeping us from something better. Not true.

On His last night, Jesus used His final words to tell His followers (then and now), "Remain in me. Unpack your bags and settle in. You won't find life anywhere else. Live in me and let me live in you. If you do, you'll blossom and bless others like never before."

And if we don't?

We won't.

71

IN

A preposition that serves to establish the relationship
of one thing to another

Therefore, there is now no condemnation for those who are
in Christ Jesus. (Romans 8:1)

As words go, *in* is always going to be "in"—*in style* and useful *in all sorts of situations.* Funny how a person can be *in the groove* one month, but *in a rut* the next. You can be *all in, in the wrong,* or *in over your head.* You can be *in debt, in the minority,* or *in a class by yourself.*

Look around and you'll see that everyone is "in" something: *in a hurry, in demand, in debt,* or *in a daze.*

Then take a few moments and consider what the Bible says about those who believe *in Christ.* (You might end up *in awe.*)

• • •

A couple things about the tiny word *in* . . . One, it's a preposition (a part of speech that expresses the relationship of one thing to another). Two, it describes a literal or figurative environment.

Something that's *in* something else is enclosed or surrounded or located within that something else. If I said, for example, "There's a ten carat diamond *in* a plastic pouch, *in* the toilet tank, *in* the restroom, *in* the Starbucks, *in* Estes Park, *in* Colorado," that would tell you a lot. (For the record, there is no such diamond—at least the last time I checked. It couldn't have been more than four carats, tops.)

Think about *in* . . . your friend who is head over heels *in love,* swimming happily *in* a sea of exciting hormones and affection. Meanwhile your neighbor is *in serious trouble* and surrounded by hard things on every side. And those who are *in Christ*? They're immersed in all that Jesus is and does.

• • •

More than two hundred times in the New Testament, we find the phrases "in Christ," "in the Lord," or "in him." This is the language of trust, relationship, intimacy . . . and ultimate security.

When we read statements like "in him was life" (John 1:4) and "in him all things hold together" (Colossians 1:17) . . . or when Scripture announces blessings like "in him we have redemption through his blood" (Ephesians 1:7) or "there is now no condemnation for those who are in Christ Jesus" (Romans 8:1), we begin to understand the wisdom of—and blessing in—obeying Jesus's command to "remain in me" (John 15:4).

• • •

Are you familiar with the old Irish prayer known as St. Patrick's Breastplate? It's a beautiful plea for protection. One section of it describes this reality of being *in Christ* (without actually using that phrase). It calls the one praying to remember:

- Christ with me
- Christ before me
- Christ behind me
- Christ in me

- Christ beneath me
- Christ above me
- Christ on my right
- Christ on my left

In other words, being surrounded in all ways by Him. Being "in Christ."

Take a moment to thank God for such astonishing truth, and to ask Him to give you the faith to believe it more deeply.

72

SHEPHERD

One who leads, protects, and provides for a flock of sheep

I am the good shepherd. The good shepherd lays down his life for the sheep.

(JOHN 10:11)

I once heard a guy ask, "What if Jesus had come to earth *this* century (instead of the first) and to some big city in the West (instead of the rural Middle East)? Might He have described himself differently? Would He perhaps have said, 'I am the good CEO' instead of 'I am the good shepherd'?"

The questioner paused and said, "I only ask because I don't know anybody who's ever even met a shepherd, much less seen one in action."

It's an intriguing question. If David were writing Psalm 23 today, would he say something like, "The Lord is my life coach" instead of "The Lord is my shepherd"?

• • •

Interesting speculations aside, David wrote when he wrote and Jesus came when He came. The biblical description is that the Lord is a *shepherd*. It might not be a familiar image, but it's beautiful and comforting. Here's why.

In Bible times, sheep were valuable, prized for their wool, milk, and meat. Therefore, a shepherd guided his flock diligently, watering and feeding them, carefully monitoring their health, and calming them whenever they got skittish. Shepherds protected their sheep from predators and other stressful situations. (Neither rams nor lambs are a match for a hungry wolf or a mountain lion, and they have a tendency to panic and become separated from the flock.)

And so the Bible likens God to a perfect shepherd (Psalm 80:1). And in this holy metaphor, God's people are compared to sheep; we're valuable, but also vulnerable.

•   •   •

My late friend Kelli knew a thing or two about shepherding. She cared for sheep for ten years. (In fact, she wrote a children's book about all the insights she gained about God being our shepherd.*)

Mostly she came to see that being a shepherd isn't like caring for a goldfish. A good shepherd, she told me once in an email exchange, is "*vigilant and responsive* in all areas of sheep life." He or she watches the weather, analyzes soil content, checks and maintains fences, procures the necessary supplies and equipment. A good shepherd closely monitors the condition of the whole flock (and its social dynamics), down to the needs of each individual sheep.

Kelli said, "And when I see that hay stored in the barn for winter, I am reminded of Jesus's faithful provision for us ahead of time, for every situation, including the ones I cannot yet see."

•   •   •

What if it's true? What if Jesus really *is* a good shepherd? What if He stands ready—today—to lead you to good places and to restore your soul and watch over it? What if He's calling you right now?

---

* Kelli Carruth Miller, *Green Grass, Still Waters* (Maitland, FL: Xulon, 2017).

Guess what . . . it *is* true. He *is* a good shepherd. We are never more secure—or more satisfied—than when we are following right behind Him.

For God's sake, and your own, listen for His voice.

73

JOY

A kind of holy happiness that can be cultivated through reveling in what is eternally true

At that time Jesus, full of joy through the Holy Spirit, said, "I praise you, Father, Lord of heaven and earth, because you have hidden these things from the wise and learned, and revealed them to little children. Yes, Father, for this is what you were pleased to do." (LUKE 10:21)

How come in so many of the Jesus movies produced over the last sixty or so years Christ isn't portrayed as being full of joy?* More times than not, He looks like a customer-service worker . . . with a bad case of the flu . . . at 4 p.m. on the day after Christmas. The on-screen Jesus is almost always somber. He has a vacant, hollow look . . . like maybe He could use some Excedrin. We can easily see this Jesus scowling at His disciples, or losing His temper with the Pharisees. It's hard to imagine Him teasing a child, or throwing back His head and laughing.

What a tragedy!

Because Jesus, as God incarnate, was joy personified.

---

* There are exceptions, of course. In Mel Gibson's *The Passion of the Christ*, there's an endearing scene of a smiling, mischievous Jesus building a table in his carpenter shop, then playfully splashing water on his mother as he washes his hands for lunch.

• • •

Both the Old and New Testament words for joy convey the idea of deep, internal gladness. At the risk of sounding cheesy, joy is the broad, steady grin of a heart that is convinced "all is well because the Father is in control." In the same way that authentic love comes ultimately from God, so also true joy—the really good stuff—originates in Him (Psalm 16:11; Zephaniah 3:17; Galatians 5:22).

Biblical joy is a far cry from the worldly happiness our culture seeks and settles for. Jesus said He, not the changing circumstances of life, is the source of joy (John 15:11). And the joy He gives is substantive, not superficial; it's enduring, not ephemeral. Though happiness quickly dissipates when bad news arrives, joy can be cultivated and kept at all times—even when one's life situation is a long way from great.

• • •

In an age dominated by bleak realities, joy is subversive. It makes commas out of the world's periods. It acts as a kind of holy defibrillator, rousing the dying with the shocking claim that things are not at all what they seem.

Though it's badly needed, joy is—sadly—rare. It's the snow leopard of the fruit of the Spirit. Far too many Christians resemble the grim Jesus of cinema or the religious people H. L. Mencken once described as "worried that somebody somewhere is having fun."

Questions: What about Christ's final prayer that His followers might be filled with His joy (John 17:13)? What about the observation of the late Warren Wiersbe that the Christian life is supposed to resemble a wedding feast, not a funeral?*

---

* Warren Wiersbe, *Meet Yourself in the Parables* (Wheaton, IL: Victor Books, 1979), 38.

● ● ●

The Bible indicates that the condition of being joyful is connected to the action of rejoicing. In other words, when we experience joy, we naturally express it. And the more joy we express, the more joy we experience.

That anonymous, wise old saint was right when he said, "Joy is a continuous, defiant 'Nevertheless.'"

Choose joy (then ask the Lord to fill you with His infinite holy gladness).

74

PEACE

The blessed calm that overwhelms a soul or relationship
when the Prince of Peace is acknowledged

Peace I leave with you; my peace I give you. I do not give to you as
the world gives. Do not let your hearts be troubled and do not be afraid.

(JOHN 14:27)

You wake up to a newsfeed as scary as any horror movie. Walking in the door at work, you instantly feel the tension of strained work relationships. Falling into bed, you toss and turn till almost midnight (then wake up at 3:50 a.m.) because you can't stop fretting about health concerns . . . or how to pay the bills . . . or your oldest child . . . or how secure your job actually is.

That's our world, isn't it? Not a very peaceful place.

How good of God to send a Prince of Peace (Isaiah 9:6)! And how kind of that prince to offer *peace* as a gift to His followers.

• • •

When Jesus talked about *peace,* He used the Hebrew word *shalom.* (If there is a more beautiful and powerful word in the Bible, it's hard to think what that would be.) Even a whispered *shalom* can calm a jittery soul.

Contrary to what some think, biblical peace doesn't merely mean the absence of conflict. No, true *shalom* also involves the presence of all things good: harmony, community, security, rest, joy, love, wholeness. Put succinctly, *shalom* is life as God meant for it to be.

Therefore, the peace that Jesus promises His followers isn't merely a fleeting feeling that things will be okay. It's a deep, abiding confidence: "All is well . . . and all will be well, because God is with me, and He's the King of everything. He's got it all—this crazy world, my precious loved ones, my dicey situation—in His big, strong, loving hands. No need, then, for me to freak out or fret. I can cast my cares on Him, relax, breathe easy, go off duty."

●　●　●

It helps to think of peace in three broad areas: *eternal* peace (the confidence that one is right with God), *external* peace (the confidence that I'm right with others), and *internal* peace (the confidence that God is with me, for me, and watching over me).

It also helps to see Jesus as the source and provider of all those kinds of peace. He reconciles sinners to God (Romans 5:1). He gives His followers the ability to be peacemakers (Matthew 5:9; Romans 12:18). Finally, He pledges to fill the hearts of His people with peace (Isaiah 26:3; Galatians 5:22; Philippians 4:6–7).

●　●　●

Take three little peace tests:

1. In your relationship with God, where are on you on the following scale?

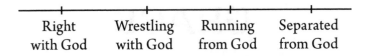

Right with God   Wrestling with God   Running from God   Separated from God

2. Where would you put your primary relationships on this scale?

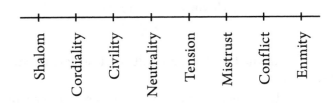

Shalom   Cordiality   Civility   Neutrality   Tension   Mistrust   Conflict   Enmity

3. Describe the condition of your heart (for example, calm, confident, apathetic, troubled, tense, anxious, panicked, terrified) as you reflect on the various areas of your life.

75

GRACE

Unmerited, unearned, undeserved favor;
kindness and love shown "just because"

Out of his fullness we have all received grace in place of
grace already given. (JOHN 1:16)

Nowhere in the four Gospels will you find Jesus saying the
word *grace.*

Instead, He just *shows* it by inviting the most unlikely people
to join His entourage . . . urging His pigheaded enemies again
and again to rethink their position . . . showing gentleness and
compassion to thieves and outcasts and sex addicts.

Jesus may not say the word *grace,* but He doles it out like a tipsy
man who just won the Powerball. He tells crazy stories about it:
Did you hear the one about the foreigner showing extreme kindness to the very man who wouldn't have given him the time of day
. . . or the one about a dad showering his foolish, selfish boy
with hugs and love rather than shame and lectures . . . or the one
about a nobleman inviting those *below* the bottom rung of the
social ladder to come to his lavish banquet?

• • •

If you've logged any time at all in church, you probably know the
word *grace* means "unmerited favor." Grace is getting something

impossibly good at precisely the moment you least deserve it. You stay out late partying, let's say, with the result that you oversleep and miss your Accounting 301 midterm. It's worth thirty percent of your semester grade. Your professor—who saw all the Instagram posts of your wild night on the town—shakes her head, sighs, and says, "Come to my office tomorrow at 4 and I'll let you take a makeup." That's grace.

Or how about this? You tell the Almighty to get lost (or worse, pretend like He doesn't exist). He responds by sending His Son to die for *you* . . . rise for *you* . . . come to *you* and say, "I want to have a relationship with *you*. I want to give *you* life to the fullest."

My friend, that's GRACE, in all caps.

• • •

We don't have a record of Jesus *saying* the word *grace*, but John—one of His closest followers—couldn't help writing about the undeserved favor Christ showed him. "Grace in place of grace already given" is the way he expressed it at the beginning of his gospel (John 1:16). What a beautiful word picture—grace like the waves at the seashore . . . undeserved blessings, rolling into and over our lives, one after another.

Perhaps as John wrote this, he thought back to that ordinary day—on the shore of the Sea of Galilee—when Jesus called *him* of all people (Matthew 4:21–22) to come and be one of His protégés. Or maybe he remembered all the times he acted like a hothead (Luke 9:54), a proud, petty jerk (Mark 10:37), or a disloyal friend (Matthew 26:56). Jesus had every reason to cut John loose. Instead, He drew him closer.

• • •

I don't know what you think you need most in your life right now, but may I suggest the grace of Jesus?

It doesn't matter what terrible things you've done. Grace sees all that—it isn't blind—and also sees all that Jesus has done, and says, "I know this sounds crazy, but you're invited to a party. And actually, *you* are the guest of honor!"

It's only when we believe that . . . and allow the grace of Jesus to enfold us, that we truly come alive.

76

TRUTH

Conformity to ultimate reality; the opposite
of falsehood and deception

Jesus answered, "I am the way and the truth and the life.
No one comes to the Father except through me." (John 14:6)

On the playground, child A calls child B a name, spits on him, shoves him—hard—to the ground, then stands over him, taunting him. Child B, tired of being bullied, grabs the basketball lying next to him. He stands up and hurls it—hard—right into the face of child A.

Want to guess what story a crying, bloody-nosed child A told the teacher? (You'll love this.) "I was standing there, and all of a sudden he just hit me in the face with the ball!"

It's not technically a lie—but it's far from the truth. Alas, this kind of selective truth telling isn't just a playground practice. Reporters sometimes do a version of this, and politicians too. CEOs, employees, spouses, and parents—we are all guilty. We get cute with the truth. We treat it like it's a commodity we can edit as we please and tailor as we see fit.

That's not at all what Jesus meant by the word.

• • •

The Old Testament word most commonly translated *truth* conveys the idea of firm, solid, or trustworthy, and it's often linked to God's faithful, covenant love for His people. Something (or someone) that's *true* is reliable. It conforms to or is consistent with ultimate reality. And ultimate reality is none other than God himself ("the God of truth" as He's called in Psalm 31:5 and Isaiah 65:16 NASB). The New Testament word echoes these ideas and also suggests certainty, authenticity.

We tend to think of *truth* as a collection of ideas or principles. Biblically, truth is rooted in and inseparable from the person of God, and in Jesus, who came into the world to show us what God is like. Long before truth is propositional, it's personal.

• • •

The world does everything with the truth but believe it. It dilutes truth, debates it, ducks it, tries to bury it. It shades it, twists it, manipulates it, and redefines it. And so we live in a culture where people speak of "fake news" and "alternate facts" . . . where they say things like, "That may be *your* truth, but it's not *my* truth."

Jesus, on the other hand, said, in effect, "Truth isn't subjective or relative or adjustable. It's not customizable or up for a vote. If it's truth you want, look at me. I'm truth personified. I will always shoot you straight. I will never deceive or mislead you. Take me or leave me."

• • •

The good thing about the one said to be "full of . . . truth," the one who said of himself, "I am the truth," is that He's also full of grace.

In other words, when He has to say truthful things to us (or about us) that aren't exactly flattering, He never does so in a way that's devastating. He tells us the whole, beautiful *gospel* truth . . . which is that we are much more sinful than we can possibly imagine and we are far more loved than we could ever dream.

77

HYPOCRITE

One who assumes a persona that's not
really who he or she is

Hypocrite! First get rid of the log in your own eye;
then you will see well enough to deal with
the speck in your friend's eye. (MATTHEW 7:5 NLT)

With aplologies to comedian Jeff Foxworthy . . .

- If you tell your kids it's wrong to lie, but then call
  in sick for work when you're not actually sick . . . you
  might be a hypocrite.
- If you look down your nose on people who are ad-
  dicted to drugs or porn or food, while you wake up every day obsessed with trying to control people and
  situations and outcomes . . . you might be a hypocrite.
- If you give a politician from the other party grief for
  infidelity, but then give a politician in your party a pass
  on the exact same behavior . . . you might
  be a hypocrite.

• • •

Redneck jokes are funny. Hypocrisy is not . . . which is surely why Jesus confronted it so harshly. Eighteen times we find the word *hypocrite* in the Gospels, always on the lips of Christ, always directed at religious people who had plastered a pious veneer over their far-from-pious hearts.

We get the word *hypocrite* directly from the Greek language. It refers to a duplicitous person, someone who pretends. Think "role" instead of "real." (This is why in ancient Greece stage actors were referred to as *hypocrites*.) A hypocrite says and does one thing here; then says and does something else there.

* * *

Everywhere He went, Jesus found himself stalked and harassed by the scribes and Pharisees, Israel's jealous, paranoid, disapproving religious leaders.

These guys had a convoluted, complicated way of interpreting God's Word. They always explained Scripture in a way that made *them* look spiritual, made everybody else look inferior, and gave them some kind of loophole or exemption from doing what God really intended.

In Matthew 23, Jesus unloaded on them. Seven times in one short exchange He called them *hypocrites*. (This, in addition to calling them "sons of hell," "blind guides," "blind fools," and "snakes"— and comparing them to "whitewashed tombs.")

Could Jesus be any clearer on how much He detests hypocrisy?

* * *

Hypocrites, Jesus called them. Actors. "Everything they do is done for men to see" (Matthew 23:5). In other words, it was all a show.

Is that a description of you right now? Are you hiding behind a religious-looking persona to cover up a messed-up soul? Are you saying all the right things but not doing them consistently?

If so, here's the good news. You don't have to continue on that road. Take off the mask and show God the truth of your heart—all the inconsistencies (He knows anyway). Confess the ugly truth. You *can* have a do-over, or at least a new chance to walk in integrity.

Jesus came to rescue sinners . . . which even includes those who are good at pretending they're not so bad.

78

WOE

An expression of grief or a pronouncement
of judgment and trouble

Woe to you, teachers of the law and Pharisees, you hypocrites!
You shut the door of the kingdom of heaven in people's faces.
You yourselves do not enter, nor will you let those enter who are trying to.
(MATTHEW 23:13)

There is a version of "Christianity" that's always peppy and sunny. Those in this camp want sermons that are relentlessly upbeat: "Let's skip over the prophets—they're too negative! And how 'bout we put the ix-nay on some of those downer psalms?"

"That Old Testament story of Elijah bringing the kid back from the dead? Perfect! But the weird story of Elisha and the two bears (the ones that mauled those forty-plus juvenile delinquents) . . . how about we eighty-six that one?"

Even Jesus gets sanitized. "Give us positive sermons about Christ's miracles and forgiveness. No one wants to hear His comments about suffering and judgment."

Individuals and churches can (and do) take this approach. It doesn't change the fact that throughout the Gospels, we see Jesus shouting the uncomfortable word, "Woe!"

• • •

Woe is an expression of grief, horror, or dread. It means "Alas!" something like "Oh no!" or "Look out!" When the Old Testament prophets said it—and they said it a lot—it meant, "Assume the crash position! Doom and gloom are just ahead!"

In the Gospels, Jesus pronounced woes on religious hypocrites (Matthew 23), on the rich and popular (Luke 6:24–26), on people who cause others to sin (Luke 17:1), on Judas (Mark 14:21), and on cities that failed to receive Him (Matthew 11:21).

● ● ●

When we hear the word *woe* on the lips of God's prophets or God's Son, we wince, but it reminds us of some important truths.

God doesn't wink at sin. In fact, if He didn't judge human wickedness, He'd cease to be holy.

Woe is never good, but it also doesn't mean the end of the world. Most of the Old Testament prophets—after describing in grim detail the terrible consequences of sin—were also careful to speak words of hope and promise . . . a kind of encouraging "Whoa!" after the discouragement of "Woe!"

Jesus, after dropping *woe* bombs left and right all across Galilee and Judea, faced the greatest woe of all. He endured the ultimate horror—death on the cross. And because He did—and emerged victorious from the grave—He's now able to offer us the wonder of eternal life.

● ● ●

Even though Christians have been redeemed *by* God and are the beloved children *of* God, we still live in a fallen world marred by sin (and its awful consequences). This means the only way to always be "up" and bubbly all the time is to live in denial.

Yes, the world is messed up. Still, we don't have to live in despair . . . don't have to walk around saying "Woe is me!" Our Savior is Christ, and He's made it so that woe's days are numbered.

79

LIGHT

The God-given illumination by which we see
physical reality and spiritual truth

The one who is the true light, who gives light to everyone,

was coming into the world. (JOHN 1:9 NLT)

I n some modern-day nativity scenes, the baby Jesus is plastic
and wired up so that he glows in the dark. In certain paintings
and stained glass windows, He appears to be incandescent. I could
be wrong on this, but I doubt that the *Son* of God was radiant like
the *sun* of God.* Had we been there for His birth I suspect we'd
have witnessed a normal-looking newborn—prunish, red-faced,
squinty-eyed.

And yet Christ did grow up and proclaim, "I am the light of
the world. Whoever follows me will never walk in darkness, but
will have the light of life" (John 8:12).

•   •   •

What is significant about this idea that Jesus is the "true light" and
that He gives "the light of life" to His followers? Three quick
thoughts about *light* . . .

---

* Except at the *transfiguration* (see chapter 64).

1. Light precedes order. When the Bible begins, the universe is described as being in chaos and engulfed in darkness. Which explains why, in just the third verse of Genesis, God creates *light* . . . in order to push back the darkness and begin the beautiful process of creation.
2. Light reveals. Portrait photographers fuss over filters and umbrella reflectors and warm fill lighting. Why? Because extremely bright light shows everything that's there (and oftentimes what's there is anything but flattering).
3. Light guides. Our swollen toes and bruised shins know this truth all too well, even if our brains tend to forget it in the dead of night.

• • •

To a world shrouded in spiritual darkness, God offered *light* that first Christmas in the person of Jesus Christ (Isaiah 9:1–2; Matthew 4:14–16). He offers that light still. For us this means two things.

Our chaotic lives have the potential to become beautiful in Christ. Jesus will, if we ask Him, come and shine the bright light of His truth into our lives and begin to order them. This process will often feel disheartening and painful. (No wonder we Christians sometimes act like spiritual cockroaches, scurrying from the light of eternal truth and hiding in the shadows!) But light is necessary. Until we see our problems clearly, we will never think to ask for help.

We can find our way home. Jesus isn't just a shepherd; He's a good shepherd with a big flashlight. William Barclay put it like this, "Without Jesus we are like men groping on an unknown road in a blackout. With him the way is clear."*

---

* William Barclay, *The Gospel of John: Volume 1* (Philadelphia: Westminster Press, 1956), 25.

• • •

The message of Christmas? To a darkened world with great hopes and even greater needs, God gave the greatest possible gift—the gift of His Son, the gift of *light*.

Are you tired of stumbling in the dark? Would you like to see? Turn to Jesus.

80

LIFE

The miraculous gift of God that animates
humans with the ability to relate physically to
creation and spiritually to their Creator

In him was life. (JOHN 1:4)

I read once that King Louis XIV would not allow his subjects to even speak the word *death* in his presence. Whether that's a historical fact or an urban legend, here is an undeniable truth: Most people, if given the power, would ban the *fact* of death—not simply the word—from human experience.

Maybe you're a death-dreader? If so, consider (again or for the first time) what Jesus had to say about *life*.

• • •

Unlike all the bloggers and podcasters who routinely tell us how to find healthier, more productive lives, the Gospels take this life discussion infinitely further and higher. They present Jesus not as some kind of enlightened life coach but as *life itself* (John 14:6). He's fully divine, they claim, one with God the Father (John 1:1, 14; 10:30; 14:9; Hebrews 1:3). This means He is the ultimate and only source of life (John 5:21, 26, 40; Colossians 3:4).*

---

* Those previous two sentences, and the verses they reference, are deserving of you closing this book for a few minutes and doing some prayerful pondering.

The New Testament actually speaks of two kinds of *life*: physical and spiritual. Physical life is pictured as the time between conception and death in which a creature enjoys organic existence and is animated with physical vitality (Luke 16:25; Genesis 23:1).

Spiritual life, on the other hand, is coming to know one's Creator (John 17:3). This new spiritual "aliveness" begins when a person is "born again" (or "born from above") through faith in Christ (John 3). It's a whole different quality of life—Jesus described it as "life . . . to the full" (John 10:10), before saying of believers, "I give them eternal life, and they shall never perish" (John 10:28). Can you believe this? We don't *attain* spiritual life; we *receive* it. It's the gift of a gracious Savior moving into our lives to make us fully alive. And—did you notice—it's endless. The one who is Life comes to stay.

●   ●   ●

Christ's wild and wonderful claims about life aside, we still face the grim reality of death. Before the month is out, if you're not showing up at some house of grief with a carb-laden casserole or an overpriced floral arrangement, you'll at least be typing on Facebook, "I'm so sorry for your loss."

What are we supposed to do about the D word?

Try this: Picture Jesus standing in the first-century version of a cemetery, telling a group of mourners, "I am the resurrection and the life" (John 11:25). Watch Him call a dead man back from the grave. A short time later, He'll exit His own—borrowed—tomb. These are previews of what awaits. They're snapshots of the coming day when graveyards will be no more, when funeral directors will need to find a new line of work.

●   ●   ●

The writer of Ecclesiastes mentioned the "insanity" that lurks in the human heart (9:3 NASB). Maybe the best example of this madness is us thinking we could turn away from the One who *is* life and expect to find what our hearts most need and want somewhere else.

81

ZACCHAEUS

The dishonest tax commissioner of Jericho whom
Jesus sought and saved and changed

Zacchaeus . . . was a chief tax collector and was wealthy. He wanted to see
who Jesus was, but because he was short he could not see over the crowd.

(LUKE 19:2–3)

In some ways, Zacchaeus is everybody who ever lived.

He enjoyed a few advantages—in his case, wealth and power. Other things in his life, however, were far from ideal. He was, to use a politically correct phrase, vertically challenged. Did Zacchaeus perhaps have a case of what would later become known as Napoleon Complex? Did he overcompensate because of his low altitude?

Alas, a short stature was the least of his problems. Because of his job (chief tax collector for the hated Roman occupiers) and the way he went about it (overcharging his neighbors and pocketing the extra) . . . well, let's just say that Zacchaeus wasn't getting a lot of friend requests on Facebook.

It seems the "wee little man" we read about in Luke 19 was equal parts empty, lonely, insecure, restless, and desperate. Lots of things in his life simply weren't working . . . which, when you think about it, is an apt description of most people on most days.

• • •

The story of Zacchaeus is ironic, comical, and symbolic, all at once. Here's the guy whose name means pure—and who is everything *but* pure. One of Jericho's most powerful men, out on a limb—literally—over Main Street.

Can you picture this scene? Zacchaeus can't get anywhere near Jesus, can't even see Him because he's so *short*...sort of like the way all individuals, because of sin, *fall short* of God's glory (Romans 3:23). Old Zac's got more money than he knows what to do with, yet he's bankrupt spiritually and socially.

Zacchaeus is the story of us all. More importantly, he's a stunning picture of how the Lord responds to us.

• • •

In John 6:44, Jesus claims that people can't/won't/don't come to Him until God first stirs their hearts and begins drawing them. This means the internal curiosity and restlessness that prompted Zacchaeus to close up his tax office for a few hours and head out in hopes of glimpsing Jesus was none other than the gracious wooing of God!

Notice that after Zacchaeus obeyed this divine nudge, Jesus came right to where he was dangling (in more ways than one). Notice that He looked right at him and called him by name (Luke 19:5). In inviting himself over to Zacchaeus's house, Jesus was essentially saying, "I want a friendship with you."

• • •

If you can read the biblical story of Zacchaeus and not come away with a big goofy grin on your face, something's dreadfully wrong.

Jesus loves empty, lonely, insecure, restless, and desperate people. That's why He came. To seek out such people . . . and to save them (Luke 19:10).

Pay attention. Can you hear Him? He's summoning you. He wants a friendship with *you*. He stands ready to forgive you and change your life. The only question is, Will you let Him?

82

HATED

To be loathed, despised, or detested

If the world hates you, keep in mind that it hated me first. If you belonged to the world, it would love you as its own. As it is, you do not belong to the world, but I have chosen you out of the world. That is why the world hates you. (JOHN 15:18–19)

If we listed the sayings of Jesus that make Christians gulp, this one would be near the top.

In short, "Count on being *hated*."

Not the kind of reassuring statement that gets turned into an eye-catching meme that believers repost and retweet.

• • •

You don't need a degree in biblical languages to understand the word *hated*.

Hate is hostility—and it's never passive. Even when haters aren't aggressively attacking the people or things they despise, they are rooting hard for their destruction.

When Jesus said the world *hated* Him, He wasn't being paranoid and He wasn't exaggerating. Wicked King Herod tried to kill Him shortly after His birth (Matthew 2:1–18). At the very beginning of His ministry, His own neighbors attempted to throw Him off a cliff (Luke 4:14–30). Before too many months passed, the

Jewish religious leaders were plotting His destruction (Mark 3:6; Luke 6:11). And the day after He made these remarks about being hated, an angry mob screamed for His death, after which executioners beat Him to within an inch of His life, then hammered Him to a Roman cross (John 18–19).

● ● ●

On the one hand, it makes no sense. Jesus "went around doing good" (Acts 10:38). He was never unkind, never a hypocrite, never took advantage of anyone. How could anyone hate Him?

On the other hand, it makes perfect sense. In the same conversation in which Jesus talked about being hated, He twice mentioned the "prince of this world" (John 14:30; 16:11). "Prince" is a reference to the devil (see chapter 11) and "world" refers to that ungodly network of structures over which the devil currently has influence. In short, this world system hates the triune God*, and everything associated with Him—His truth, His plan, and His people. So when Jesus came as a Light into that dark, evil world, unrepentant people hated Him. After all, He exposed who and what they really were (John 3:19–20).

● ● ●

Jesus said it, and the rest of the New Testament echoes it: If we identify as followers of Christ, we'll be despised by the world too. We'll suffer persecution (2 Timothy 3:12).† This is actually an everyday experience for most believers around the world. For some reason, believers in America still act surprised (even

---

* Do unredeemed people really *hate* God? The Bible says they do (Deuteronomy 5:9; 32:41; Psalms 68:1; 81:15; 139:21).

† The persecution can range from verbal abuse, social ostracism, and discrimination in education and employment (in the West) to more extreme mistreatment in other parts of the world: confiscation of property, physical beatings, torture, rape, slavery, imprisonment, and execution.

outraged) when the animosity that Jesus said we should expect actually comes our way.

If being hated is our destiny, let's at least be hated for the right reason—because people see the grace-filled, truth-filled life of Jesus (John 1:14) on display in our lives.

Let's *not* be hated for claiming to be His followers but then living lives that bear no resemblance to His.

83

HOSANNA

An exclamation asking the Lord to save

Those who went ahead and those who followed shouted, "Hosanna!"
"Blessed is he who comes in the name of the Lord!" (MARK 11:9)

Growing up in the New Orleans suburbs, I could never get jazzed* about the Macy's Thanksgiving Day Parade or the New Year's Day Rose Parade mostly because, well, we had Mardi Gras.† Even though our floats didn't literally float, and even though they weren't made of gorgeous flowers, they featured costumed riders who showered us parade-goers with beaded necklaces, doubloons, and other goodies.‡ All we had to do was wave and yell continuously, "Throw me something, mister!"

• • •

The closest thing to a parade in the life of Christ was His triumphal entry into Jerusalem the final week of His life (Matthew 21:1–11; Mark 11:1–11; Luke 19:28–44; John 12:12–19).

---

* Do you see what I did there? Pun intended.
† And also because in the mid 1960s, if I wanted to watch one of those other parades, I had to do it on a black-and-white television about the size of a toaster. (Hard to make *anything* look very exciting on equipment like that.)
‡ At the famous Zulu Mardi Gras parade in New Orleans, the greatest prize is a decorated coconut. These are handed out, rather than thrown, for obvious reasons.

In this procession, there were no flowery floats, no marching bands from Jerusalem U, no song-and-dance numbers, no fez-wearing Shriners driving tricked-out go-carts and motorcycles. Just a solitary young man on a young donkey.

Even though Jesus didn't throw anything to anyone, the mood of the crowd was jubilant. Onlookers—instead of hollering, "Throw me something!"—yelled the Hebrew word *Hosanna*, a hopeful, confident exclamation. Its meaning is seen in Psalm 118:25 in the petition, "O LORD, do save, we beseech You" (NASB).

• • •

Some background is helpful. From ancient times, Psalm 118 has been sung or recited by the Jewish people at their annual Feast of Tabernacles. Also known as Sukkot and the Festival of Booths, this early harvest celebration is essentially the Jewish Thanksgiving. It involves erecting and living in makeshift huts and waving palm branches (Leviticus 23:39–43) to celebrate and commemorate God's faithfulness during their years of wilderness wandering after leaving Egypt.

This is why the crowds yelled "Hosanna!" and waved palm branches as Christ rode past. They were expressing the fervent hope, at least in that moment, that He was, as He claimed, the Messiah, the one the prophets said would come and save.

• • •

The word *Hosanna* isn't part of our everyday discourse, but perhaps it should be. As I point out in *Spiritual Life Hacks*, the salvation that God wants us to experience isn't merely historical (something that happened to you, say, back in the fourth grade) or eventual (something you get when you die). It's rescue *now*!

"God can save us today—and in the most practical ways. Whether you whisper it or shout it, crying out 'Hosanna!' to Jesus is an acknowledgment of two personal truths: *I am a mess who happens to be in a mess,* and *I believe you can deliver me.*"[*]

[*] Len Woods, *Spiritual Life Hacks* (Eugene, OR: Harvest House, 2019), 37.

84

SPIT

To project saliva out of one's mouth

He took the blind man by the hand and led him outside the village.
When he had spit on the man's eyes and put his hands on him,
Jesus asked, "Do you see anything?" (MARK 8:23)

Most people lump saliva in with landfills and sewage treat-ment plants—a necessary thing but not something they really want to see or think about.

But then Jesus comes along—God incarnate, if we take the Bible at face value—and, what do you know, He's both spitting and being spit upon!

What can *spit* possibly show us about the Son of God?

• • •

The two primary Greek words translated *spit* in our English Bibles are *ptuo* (which explains where we get our exclamation *Ptooey!*— what we say when we're pretending to spit) and *emptuo* (which is self-explanatory . . . spitting is emptying your mouth of its saliva by projecting it outwardly, instead of swallowing it).

Definitions aside, spitting is, well, nasty! When a grandparent with dementia expectorates on the carpet or a preschooler angrily sprays his sister with saliva, we gag.

And yet here's Jesus using spit for holy purposes. He restores a mute man's ability to speak by spitting—perhaps even putting His spit *on* the man's tongue (Mark 7:31–37)! In one place He restores the sight of a blind man by spitting "on the man's eyes" (Mark 8:23). Elsewhere a sightless soul finds healing when Jesus spits on the ground, makes mud, puts the mixture on the man's eyes, and tells him to go wash it off (John 9:6).

And after Jesus finishes spitting His way through Galilee and Judea, showing the shocking love of God, He faces the indignity of soldiers and religious leaders spitting in His face with absolute disdain and disgust (Matthew 26:67; 27:30).

• • •

Did you know your saliva has an upside? Not only does it contain your genetic blueprint, it also fights tooth decay, helps you digest your food, and contains antibodies that speed healing (which is why a cut in your mouth heals more quickly than a cut on your hand).

The ancients believed in saliva's medicinal qualities, which may explain why Jesus sometimes spat before healing people.

As to why God incarnate would knowingly allow sinners to humiliate Him, by showering Him with their spit and disgust, we can only shrug. We know the final answer is love, but the *reasons* for such love remain a mystery.

• • •

Another way we could describe God's desire to make us like His Son (see Romans 8:29; Galatians 4:19) is to say He wants us to become "the spitting image"—insert rim shot—of Jesus.

In all seriousness, such transformation is possible. Even if we keep our saliva to ourselves (highly recommended!), we can pray for and work for the healing of others. And when unbelievers spit at us—whether venomous, angry words, mocking comments, or even, God forbid, actual saliva—we can endure with dignity and grace. We don't have to get spitting mad and fire back.

85

CRUCIFIED

To be affixed to an upright stake and left
to die a slow, agonizing death

Then he released Barabbas to them. But he had Jesus flogged,
and handed him over to be crucified. (MATTHEW 27:26)

The Passion of the Christ, Mel Gibson's 2004 film about the final hours of Jesus's life before His death on the cross, sold a bunch of tickets . . . and sparked a bunch of conversation and controversy.

Some have pointed out that the Gospels simply say that Jesus was "flogged, and . . . crucified" (*without* describing those cruel practices in excruciating detail). And yet, they note, Gibson's film spends most of its 127 minutes fixated on Christ's suffering.

David Edelstein of *Slate* magazine called *The Passion of the Christ* a "bloody mess." Critic Roger Ebert gave it a thumbs up, but cautioned in an interview with MSNBC's Deborah Norville, "It should be rated 'NC-17.' It's the most violent movie that I've ever seen."*

• • •

Whether we think Gibson went overboard with the gore, a couple facts are indisputable: In the first century, flogging was a ghastly

---

* "Roger Ebert on 'The Passion of the Christ,'" MSNBC on NBC News, February 26, 2004. http://www.nbcnews.com/id/4377605/ns/msnbc-deborah_norville_tonight/t/roger-ebert-pas sion-christ/#.Xy9gyxNKjjA.

form of torture, and crucifixion was the worst possible way to die. The Greek verb translated *crucify* is from the same root word as the noun *cross*. It means "to put on a stake or post." In the Roman Empire, condemned criminals either were impaled directly on a upright stake, or they were affixed to a crossbeam (by either rope or nails) and then, with that crossbeam, attached either to the top of a stake (picture a capital T) or fastened to the middle of a stake (picture a + sign).

In both cases, gravity would make it increasingly difficult for a victim to draw breath. Crucifixion was death by slow suffocation, while bloodthirsty onlookers jeered, laughed, and pointed.

● ● ●

It's stunning to read the Gospels and realize that Jesus knew in advance He was going to be crucified, yet nobody had to drag him, kicking and screaming, to His death. He went willingly.

There's an old joke that most condemned criminals are innocent—and if you don't believe it, just ask them. In this case, Jesus truly *was* innocent (Pilate even said so himself on three different occasions). But you won't find Christ getting an attorney to file a last-minute appeal with the Fifth Circuit Court.

Jesus was *not* a victim. He was living out the very script *He* had written. He was on a mission. He had been born to die. He was destined for the cross.

● ● ●

It seems crazy, doesn't it? The idea that unspeakable violence against God could actually lead to peace with God—that because an innocent man endured crucifixion, guilty people can experience justification?* That out of the evil and horror of death on a cross emerges the hope of a beautiful new life?

---

* Justification is the act of being declared righteous; it's being in right standing with God.

No wonder the apostle Paul later exulted, "For the message of the cross is foolishness to those who are perishing, but to us who are being saved it is the power of God" (1 Corinthians 1:18).

86

INSCRIPTION

A sign or written notice that bears a title

Pilate also wrote an inscription and put it on the cross.
It was written, "JESUS THE NAZARENE, THE KING OF THE JEWS."
(JOHN 19:19 NASB)

The Roman orator and writer Cicero called crucifixion "the cruelest and foulest of punishments."

The Gospels confirm this grim assessment. In first-century Jerusalem, Roman crosses were raised at a well-trafficked location (Matthew 27:39; Mark 15:29) appropriately known as "the place of the skull."

Often lost amid all the physical violence was a simple administrative custom: the writing of an *inscription* (to be affixed above the head of the condemned). Its purpose? To spell out for onlookers the identity of the crucified and the crime that warranted such a ghastly fate.

• • •

The Greek word translated "inscription" (it's rendered "notice" in the NIV; "sign" in the NLT) is *titlos,* the source of our English word *title.* An inscription was essentially a caption meant to explain the whole grim scene unfolding beneath it.

According to Pilate, the crime of "Jesus the Nazarene" was being "King of the Jews." Pilate's placard was meant to serve as both reminder (*There is no king but Caesar*) and warning (*This is what happens to those who challenge Rome's authority*). The sign was also intended to humiliate the occupied Jews: "Hey, you religious weirdos, behold your King! Some king." The inscription horrified the Jewish leaders, who had summarily rejected Jesus. "Don't write that he's our king!" the chief priest protested. "Write that he *claimed* to be our king!"

Surprisingly, Pilate (who usually tried to keep everyone happy so he could keep his job) refused. "What I have written, I have written" (John 19:22).

• • •

Pilate wrote his inscription in three languages (John 19:20)— ostensibly so that everyone might get the joke. It was in Hebrew, the language of the Jews; Latin, the language used in government circles; and Greek, the everyday vernacular across the empire.

This is one of history's most ironic moments. A few hours earlier Pilate had been asking, "What is truth?" Now, he's unwittingly proclaiming the greatest truth ever: the crucified, bloody ragdoll of a man, with eyes swollen shut, is, in fact, the King of the Jews. And to hear Christ tell it, King of the Gentiles too, King of all there is . . . you, me, everything.

• • •

Can the inscription really be true? The man's not seated on a throne; He's nailed to a cross. It's a crucifixion, not a coronation. Rather than wearing a golden crown dripping with jewels, Jesus sports a crown of thorns dripping with His own blood. And instead of being surrounded by adoring subjects, He is mocked by sinners and situated between a couple lowly criminals.

The gospel portrait is of a most unkingly King. But look at the inscription again and consider another gospel truth: things are rarely what they seem.

87

CLOTHES

Garments worn to cover one's nakedness

And they crucified him. Dividing up his clothes,
they cast lots to see what each would get. (MARK 15:24)

Y ou're walking down a busy street when it hits you: "I'm not
wearing any clothes!" Or you're standing backstage, in the
wings of a theater, when someone suddenly shoves you out into
the spotlight. As the audience gasps, you realize, *I'm buck naked!*

Relax! These are only dreams (I hope!). Experts who study
such things say these sorts of dreams are common because most
people have a subconscious fear of being exposed, of being seen
as they truly are, and consequently, of being mocked or humiliated. For every exhibitionist who likes to parade around in the
buff, there are a thousand (or more) modest souls who deeply
believe that "Clothing covers a multitude of sins."

Given all this, how come Jesus is naked up there on the cross?

• • •

Once the soldiers hammered Jesus to the cross, the Gospels show
them gambling for His garments.[*]

---

[*] John notes in his gospel (19:24) that, without even realizing it, these pagan soldiers were fulfilling the messianic prophecy found in Psalm 22:18.

Artists through the centuries have always opted to be discreet—giving Jesus a loincloth as He suffers on the cross. But most historians are convinced the Romans stripped their victims bare. They did this to add insult to injury, to inflict not just physical pain but also maximum emotional humiliation.

Think about Christ in these moments, naked in front of a crowd of jeering onlookers. With His arms nailed to the cross, He cannot cover up. And then remember this: He came here knowingly and willingly. Why?

• • •

The only place in the Bible where nakedness isn't connected to fear and shame is in Genesis 2, before the fall. In Eden, Adam and Eve didn't have to spend a penny on clothing. Completely exposed, they felt zero shame. This is because they were other-centered, fully known, and unconditionally accepted. The concept of rejection wasn't yet a thing.

But the moment they turned away from God, everything unraveled. Their self-absorbed souls filled with guilt, fear, and shame. They frantically covered up with fig leaves . . . then jumped into the bushes! And humanity has been covering up ever since. We do our best to hide our flaws and failures and insecurities behind the modern-day fig leaf of a carefully curated public image.

• • •

Wouldn't it be wonderful to be free from the fear of being emotionally, spiritually naked? Imagine no longer feeling that uneasy sense of shame at the core of your being.

The gospel of Jesus says we can be free. Come to the cross and look.

Do you see the Savior stripped naked there? Behold God's merciful heart. If anyone deserves to be exposed and humiliated, it's us. If anyone deserved to be exalted and honored, it's Jesus. But He took our place. He took our sin—and the terrible shame of it—upon himself. He suffered the misery of being exposed. Why? So that we might receive the mercy of being clothed in His righteousness. What a picture of the heart of God! Jesus was willing to be stripped bare, so that we might be covered in His forgiveness and love.

This is one of the most attractive qualities of a follower of Jesus who is learning to live a gospel-centered, cross-focused life. Shame loses its power. Instead of unease at the core of our being, there is increasing peace. We can be authentic. We find increasing freedom from the pressure to hide, to impress, to pretend to be better than others.

88

CURTAIN

The veil that stood in front of the most holy place
in the Jewish temple

The curtain of the temple was torn in two from top to bottom. (MARK 15:38)

In the heart of the sprawling temple complex in Jerusalem, where Jesus spent so much time teaching His followers (and sparring with the Pharisees), were two areas that were off limits to everyone but Israel's priests. The outer area was called "the holy place." There, appointed priests regularly maintained the golden lampstand, burned incense, and placed consecrated bread before the Lord.

The innermost room was like the reactor building in a nuclear power plant—highly restricted and extremely dangerous. Called "the most holy place" (or "holy of holies"), this was the one place on earth where God Almighty had said to His chosen people, "I will meet with you" (Exodus 30:6).

Because God manifested His glory in this place, it stayed hidden behind a massive veil or *curtain*.

• • •

The Greek word for *curtain* literally means "that which spreads out downwards." Scholars agree that the veil in the temple did this in a big way. It was, perhaps, two to three inches thick, thirty feet wide, and sixty feet tall. It was woven of multicolored thread and decorated with cherubim (2 Chronicles 3:14).

The priests ministering in the holy place could see the curtain; they dared not go behind it. Only Israel's high priest could enter the most holy place . . . and that knee-knocking experience happened just once a year, on the Day of Atonement (Exodus 30:10; Hebrews 9:7).

In effect, this curtain served as a constant reminder of the dilemma of sinful people attempting to draw near to a holy God. It was glorious and ominous, hinting at life, warning of death.

● ● ●

The first three gospels all declare the same startling fact. When Jesus breathed His last on the cross, this heavy linen barrier suddenly ripped in two. Matthew and Mark add "from top to bottom," suggesting, not-so-subtly, that the source of this miraculous tearing was above us.

Here's how the writer to the Hebrews describes the supernatural event: "Therefore, brothers and sisters . . . we have confidence to enter the Most Holy Place by the blood of Jesus, by a new and living way opened for us through the curtain, that is, his body" (Hebrews 10:19–20).

The original readers of these words would have fallen out of their chairs. Through Christ crucified, anyone can approach God. As Christ's body was torn, the curtain was torn. By His willingness to endure the scourging, the brutal beatings, the nails, He opened forever and for all who believe a way of access to God.

● ● ●

Maybe because of choices you've made, you're avoiding God. It's as if a big, thick veil of guilt and shame hangs between you and your heavenly Father . . . May I restate the promise of the torn curtain? God isn't angry with you! Jesus has dealt with your sins! Because of His sacrifice, His torn flesh, you can draw near. The way is open, and God invites you in.

Don't trust your feelings. Trust what Jesus did at the cross. The torn curtain of history says we are welcome in God's presence. Any day. Any time.

89

EARTHQUAKE

A geologic disturbance that causes shaking
and trembling (in the ground and in the heart)

When the centurion and those with him who were guarding Jesus saw the
earthquake and all that had happened, they were terrified, and exclaimed,
"Surely he was the Son of God!" (MATTHEW 27:54)

Strange things happened while Jesus hung on the cross:

- The sky went utterly black for three hours (Matthew 27:45)!
- The curtain (see previous chapter) in the innermost
  part of the temple ripped in two from top to bottom
  (Matthew 27:51)!
- An *earthquake* shook Jerusalem (Matthew 27:51)!

Oftentimes, in the days after an earthquake, scientists record smaller tremors called aftershocks. However, following the earthquake that rattled Jerusalem on Good Friday came an even bigger one on Sunday morning (Matthew 28:2). It was so powerful it shook the entire world, figuratively speaking. Twenty centuries later it continues to jolt people.

• • •

The Greek word translated *earthquake* in the New Testament is the word that gives us our English words *seismograph* and *seismologist*.

In simple terms, an earthquake is a seismic event that's impossible to miss, a geological shuddering within the earth's crust.

Smaller earthquakes rattle windows and nerves. Larger earthquakes can sometimes topple structures and reshape whole landscapes.

• • •

Among the four gospel writers, only Matthew mentions the Good Friday earthquake. This tremor (with its aftershocks) was so intense, it struck fear in the hearts of the Roman soldiers who were on crucifixion duty. Perhaps Matthew mentions it because his gospel is the "most Jewish" of the four, and to the Jewish mind earthquakes were viewed as a sign of God's judgment (see Isaiah 29:6).

In truth, the death of Christ *was* a judgment of sin. Not only that, it was a payment *for* sin, and a victory *over* sin. Thus the physical earthquake that rocked the earth at the time of Christ's death was an announcement of world-shaking spiritual realities: the collapse of an old religious system and the rise of a new and perfect way. In a real sense, Christ's sacrifice resulted in a violent shaking of the spiritual status quo.

• • •

If you've never personally experienced an earthquake, small ones feel like a quick jolt followed by several strong shakes that pass quickly. Quakes on the top end of the Richter scale are marked by a much larger jolt, followed by violent shaking that can last anywhere from a few seconds to a couple of minutes. In larger quakes, the USGS warns, "It will be difficult to stand up. The contents of your house will be a mess."*

Spiritual earthquakes are like that too, the difference being that we can always count on God to bring blessing out of all that shaking.

---

* See the USGS website, "What does an earthquake feel like?," https://www.usgs.gov/faqs /what-does-earthquake-feel?qt-news_science_products=0#qt-news_science_products.

90

GARDEN

A green space set aside for agricultural
or recreational purposes

At the place where Jesus was crucified, there was a garden, and in the garden
a new tomb, in which no one had ever been laid. (JOHN 19:41)

According to the Good Book, human life as we know it be-gan in a pristine *garden*, planted by the Lord God himself (Genesis 2:8–16). Read the Bible to the end and you'll see that God is preparing a *garden-like city* for all the redeemed. (This explains John Milton's famous two-poem summary of the great story of God and humanity: *Paradise Lost* and *Paradise Regained.*[*])

In the last chapter of the final book of the Bible, the apostle John sees a river full of the "water of life" (Revelation 22:1–2)—reminiscent of the ancient river that flowed in Eden (Genesis 2:10). Along the banks of this eternal waterway, John sees "the tree of life," a reference that causes the hearts of alert Bible readers to race. Access to this tree was forbidden when our original ancestors turned away from God (Genesis 3:22–24)!

And in between these once and future gardens? We see Jesus frequenting *other* gardens.

• • •

---

[*] The word *paradise* comes from the Persian language. It means "park" or "forest."

Garden in the Bible means the same thing that *garden* in our world means. It's a plot of land, a green space, often surrounded by a wall and earmarked for agricultural or recreational use (1 Kings 21:2; Esther 1:5; Jeremiah 29:5). Sometimes burial plots were located within gardens (2 Kings 21:18).

Gethsemane is the famous garden on the Mount of Olives where Jesus agonized in prayer the night before He died. In the place He was crucified there was another garden. That's where a wealthy man named Joseph of Arimathea owned a tomb. That tomb is where Jesus was buried, but only for one weekend (John 19:41–42).

• • •

It's no coincidence that Jesus spent part of His last day, and the brief hours of His death, in gardens. The first man defied his Creator in the garden of Eden; therefore, it was only fitting that the God-man yield to His heavenly Father in the garden of Gethsemane.

And since a garden was where Adam brought death into the world, a garden was where Jesus went to defeat death.

• • •

A funny thing happened when Jesus rose from the dead. Mary Magdalene showed up at the garden tomb, saw that Jesus's body was gone, and her first thought was, *Grave robbers!* Overcome with emotion, she turned, looked straight at Jesus . . . and didn't recognize Him. He asked her two questions . . . and she still didn't grasp His identity. She assumed He was the gardener (John 20:15).

We smile at her confusion. But in a sense, she was spot on. Jesus *is* the ultimate Gardener. Who else has the ability to take our barren hearts and our weed-infested world, and turn them into verdant places bursting with life?

91

RISEN

To be awakened, restored, or raised to life

"Don't be alarmed," [the angel] said. "You are looking for Jesus the
Nazarene, who was crucified. He has risen! He is not here.
See the place where they laid him." (MARK 16:6)

Never mind that Jesus—on several occasions—talked matter-of-factly about rising from the dead.* Somehow His disciples were flabbergasted when it happened.

Admit it . . . don't you find it a *little* odd that the enemies of Jesus couldn't forget His resurrection promises (see Matthew 27:63) . . . while the followers of Jesus couldn't remember them? Among the remaining eleven, wouldn't you think at least *one* might have said, "Guys, the Lord told us repeatedly He was going to rise after three days. Plus we watched Him bring Jairus's daughter back from the dead . . . AND the son of that widow from Nain . . . AND Lazarus. So, I don't know about the rest of you knuckleheads, but *I'm* camping out in the garden, close to that tomb. *I'm* going to wait and watch. What else do we have to do?"

• • •

---

* See Matthew 17:22–23; 20:18–19; 26:32; Mark 9:31; 10:33–34; 14:28; and Luke 9:44.

"He has *risen!*" the angel announced, using a common word that usually means "to get up, or awaken"—but can also mean "to rise from the dead, to be resurrected."

It's important to remember that *resurrection* as modeled by Jesus isn't *resuscitation* (being revived only to die again). And it's not *reincarnation* (one's soul migrating to another body). It's the ultimate remaking of our body and reuniting it with our soul. Resurrection leads to a physical, embodied state. It is the reversal of death, forever.

• • •

In non-Jewish cultures, Greek dualism was the prevailing philosophy. It taught that the physical, material world was bad and that spiritual, immaterial reality was good. The body therefore was inferior—a prison, if you will. So "salvation" involved being liberated from the confines of the physical. No Greek dualist, once delivered from the body by death, would want to be reunited with his or her body. That idea—of resurrection—would have been undesirable, unthinkable, distasteful. Some kind of existence after death, yes! But not bodily resurrection.

Even for the Jews living at the time of Christ, resurrection was seen as an event destined to take place at the end of history, for all the righteous. It was part of the final, divine restoration of all things. It was not a private, personal happening to one individual in the midst of history. The Jews just didn't have a category for that.

All of which prompts the question, In an antiresurrection culture, why make such a claim central to your message? Yet the apostles did! The resurrection, C. H. Dodd noted, "is not a belief that grew up within the church; it is the belief around which the church itself grew up."*

• • •

---

* C. H. Dodd, *The Founder of Christianity*, chapter 9, Religion Online, accessed December 3, 2020, religion-online.org/book-chapter/chapter-9-the-story-iii-the-sequel/.

When they saw the empty tomb and later the resurrected Jesus, the disciples eagerly began spreading the word that "Christ has risen!" And when push came—not to shove but to martyrdom— many of Christ's followers died insisting upon His resurrection. The resurrection of Jesus wasn't a legend or theological doctrine that developed over many years and then got propagated much later. It was news that circulated widely *during the lifetime of the people who lived through these events* (see 1 Corinthians 15:3–4).

Because Christ is risen, we have ultimate hope in a world filled with caskets and crematoriums. Death isn't the end. Life gets the last word, the last (eternal) laugh.

92

DOUBT

To be at odds within oneself; to waver internally
between belief and unbelief

Then the eleven disciples went to Galilee, to the mountain
where Jesus had told them to go. When they saw him, they worshiped
him; but some doubted. (MATTHEW 28:16–17)

What are we to make of *this* passage?

Jesus's most devoted followers were gathered in Galilee. Matthew—one of the eleven at this mandated mountain-side meeting—informs us that when Christ appeared, "they saw him" and—understandably—"they worshiped" the resurrected Lord. Then Matthew adds a curious detail: "but some doubted."

Does it disturb you or encourage you that even the apostles had faith struggles —*while staring at the resurrected Christ?*

• • •

The Greek verbs translated *doubt* in the New Testament mean "to waver back and forth in one's mind" or "to separate, in the sense of having a divided mind."

Such great word pictures! Doubt is the nonstop tug-of-war in our hearts between belief and unbelief. Doubt comes and goes because, well, faith ebbs and flows.

Some days eternal realities seem so tangible, we think, "Why can't *everyone* see this? Why doesn't *everyone* trust God . . . all the time?" Other moments . . . or days . . . or even seasons, we struggle fiercely to believe the most basic truths about God. Perhaps this is the reason the apostle Paul urged his young protégé Timothy to "fight the good *fight of faith*" (1 Timothy 6:12 NASB; emphasis added).

Faith *is* a fight. It's a lifelong war. Unconvinced? Ask Peter how quickly one can go from walking *on* the sea to nearly drowning *in* it (Matthew 14:31). Ask John the Baptist how trials can torpedo the trust you thought was bulletproof (Luke 7:18–23). Or talk to Thomas about his famous faith struggles (John 20:24–29).

• • •

The old joke is that 90 percent of all Christians admit to having doubts, and the other 10 percent lie about their struggles to take God at His word. Funny, sad, and true.

Jesus's gracious interactions with His disciples show us that doubting isn't unusual, nor is it the unpardonable sin. Ever notice that right on the heels of the disciples' odd faith struggle in Matthew 28, Jesus instructed them to "go and make disciples of all nations"? This was His way of saying, "If you think that I'm done with you because you're having a faith hiccup, think again."

Every believer has struggles believing. We all doubt. (This is why, in addition to stirring "faith chapters" like Hebrews 11, the Bible also contains "doubt passages" like Psalm 88.) In truth, every sin we ever commit is rooted in doubt—doubt that God's word is true or that His ways are wise or best. Think about it: If we always trusted God completely, we'd never sin.

• • •

Is your faith shaky? Maybe you don't doubt God's *existence*, but rather His *wisdom* . . . His *power* . . . or His *care* for you. If so, ponder the question of Jesus, "Where is your faith?" (Luke 8:25). Then pray the honest prayer of the unnamed man in Mark 9:24, "I believe; help my unbelief" (ESV).

And if you've got friends or loved ones who are struggling to believe, keep this verse close: "Be merciful to those who doubt" (Jude 22).

93

APOSTLE

A person sent out (with the full authority of the one doing the sending) to be a special messenger

When morning came, he called his disciples to him and chose twelve of them, whom he also designated apostles. (Luke 6:13)

First you watch a snippet from the White House press secretary's daily briefing. Changing channels, you listen to the spokesman of a big chemical company talk about a mysterious explosion at one of its plants. Another click and you hear a story about a team of negotiators who have been sent to the Middle East by their governments to hammer out a ceasefire agreement.

Who knew when you turned on your TV set, you'd get to see a bunch of apostles?

• • •

Our word *apostle* comes from the Greek verb that means "to send." The New Testament uses the word in at least two ways. Primarily it's used to refer to the handful of disciples Jesus handpicked to be His special assistants, then authorized to be His envoys (Mark 6:30). In this case, the word (think Apostle, capital *A*) refers more to a foundational office of the church (Ephesians 2:20). The twelve, along with other Apostles like Paul (Galatians 1:15–17) and Barnabas (Acts 14:14) and James (Galatians 1:19), functioned in the first century much like Moses and the prophets did in ancient Israel. That is to say, they were selected by God to lead the people of God and declare the truth of God.

The New Testament uses the word *apostle* (think lowercase *a*) in a secondary way—to designate special representatives appointed by the Apostles (and other leaders of the church) to deliver specific messages or gifts (2 Corinthians 8:23; Philippians 2:25). Throughout the New Testament we see congregations sending out special envoys for such purposes.

In Hebrews 3:1, Jesus is called an Apostle. If anyone deserves the title, the ultimate Messenger with the ultimate Message surely does.

● ● ●

It's important to remember the sequence. Before Jesus designated the twelve disciples as apostles and sent them out to preach the good news (see Matthew 10), they first had to immerse themselves in the other part of their job description which was simply to "be with him" (Mark 3:14). Most New Testament scholars agree that during those first months of following Jesus, the disciples mainly tagged along, listened, and watched. Only after some time had elapsed (perhaps as much as a year) did Jesus send out the twelve on any kind of mission trip.

In other words, "Come follow and learn!" preceded "Go and tell!" This is because someone has to know who Jesus is and what He's said before he or she can effectively go anywhere and speak for Him.

● ● ●

How encouraging is that? Jesus called flawed, messed-up people to come and be His disciples. Then, as He slowly transformed them, He sent them out to show others how to become followers.

As apostles (little *a*) in training, this isn't a bad prayer for us to pray: "Lord, to whom do you want to send me to deliver your message? Where would you like me to go?"

94

AGAIN

An adverb that suggests repeated action (and that echoes the gospel when found on the lips of Jesus)

If I go and prepare a place for you, I will come again and receive you to Myself, that where I am, there you may be also. (JOHN 14:3 NASB)

I s there a better word than *again*?

- She said she'd like to go out ... *again.*
- Your child made the honor roll ... *again.*
- Your year-end bonus was bigger than you expected ... *again.*

Is there a more discouraging word than *again*?

- The insurance company denied you ... *again.*
- The baby has an ear infection ... *again.*
- You did that thing (that you swore you *wouldn't* do) ... *again.*

• • •

The Greek adverb translated "again" (more than one hundred times) in the New Testament means "once more." It's the idea of repeating an action.

In the Gospels, we see Jesus repeatedly doing good things: traveling again and again to where needy people were (Mark 2:13; 3:1; 7:31; 11:27; John 4:46); patiently announcing God's truth again and again; assuring His nervous disciples (as the time of His death drew near) that they would see Him again (John 16:16–22), because He would come again (John 14:3)!

The people in the Gospels are a different story:

- The Jewish leaders getting infuriated with Jesus again and again (John 10:31, 39).
- The disciples falling asleep again and again when Jesus asked them to stay awake and pray (Matthew 26:36–46).
- Peter denying again and again that he knew Jesus (Matthew 26:72; John 18:27).
- The crowd calling again and again for Jesus's crucifixion (Luke 23:21).

• • •

When referencing our behavior or circumstances, *again* often has a bleak effect. We sin again or troubles come again. In such moments, it's easy to doubt—again—that we're God's children, or wonder—again—if He is really good.

Those are the times we need the other meaning of the word *again*. (I'm referring to those places in the New Testament where it conveys the idea of "on the other hand.")

Yes, it might be true that you failed or that life is hard. But then again (on the other hand), that's not the only truth in town.

• • •

The word *again*—used so often *by* Jesus and in descriptions *of* him—is a gospel word. It suggests persistence (and love). In it, we see the Lord's dogged determination to always go the extra mile, to come back once more. The again of Jesus doesn't obsess over what happened yesterday. It's gracious and forward-looking. It says, "Now is the only moment that matters."

Put your hope in this glorious truth: the redemptive *agains* of Jesus are bigger than your regrettable ones.

95

GO

To leave where you are

Therefore go and make disciples of all nations, baptizing them in the name of the Father and of the Son and of the Holy Spirit. (MATTHEW 28:19)

If the ministry of Jesus shows us anything it is that the spiritual life is fundamentally about *movement*.

We respond to the gracious call of Christ by "coming" to Him. (This is the learning, training component of discipleship.) As we follow Him, there are times Christ nudges us to *go* on little missions for Him. (This is the serving, shining, sharing side to discipleship.)

Healthy, well-rounded believers engage in both of these movements, participating in this ongoing rhythm. Coming and going. Maturing and ministering. Becoming a disciple and making disciples. It's by coming to Jesus that our own lives are altered. It's by going on mission for Him that the world is changed.

• • •

The imperative verb *go* is the command to be off, to depart, to leave, to move along. When Jesus tells people to go (which He does a lot), it invariably means, "Don't just sit there! I have an important task I want you to do":

- "Go and be reconciled" (Matthew 5:24).
- "Go, show yourself to the priest" (Matthew 8:4).
- "Go . . . and report to John what you hear and see" (Matthew 11:4).
- "Go, sell your possessions . . . come, follow me" (Matthew 19:21).
- "Go home . . . and tell them how much the Lord has done for you" (Mark 5:19).

When we *go* as the Lord prompts us, good things happen; God is honored, others are blessed, and we experience the joy of obedience and service.

• • •

Some Christians think that "going" for Christ necessarily involves realtors and shipping crates, visas and foreign-language training. It certainly *can* mean all that (and every believer should be open to the possibility of relocating, perhaps even overseas). But for most followers of Jesus, the command to *go* means something far less dramatic but equally important: *going* into the break room and asking a couple coworkers to go eat lunch, *going* across the cul-de-sac to meet the new neighbors, or *going* on your granddaughter's fourth-grade field trip as a chaperone.

• • •

Spend thirty seconds scanning the news headlines and you just might conclude the world is hopeless, that *going* and doing anything for Jesus is too risky and messy.

Three true things: (1) People are messy (including us)! (2) The world is far from hopeless. And (3) The gospel is "the power of God that brings salvation to everyone who believes" (Romans 1:16).

Since the life of faith is about movement, and since the first two letters of gospel are "go," how about moving (literally, today) from where you are . . . toward someone God has put near you?

96

RIGHTEOUS ONE

A title of Jesus that describes His sinless character
and perfect obedience to God's law

Then he said: "The God of our ancestors has chosen you to know
his will and to see the Righteous One and to hear words from his mouth."

(ACTS 22:14)

If the opposite of right is wrong, then it would follow that a *righteous* person is free from wrong. Imagine that: a spotless character. No corrupt motives or impure thoughts. No giving in to inappropriate impulses. Never spouting a sinful word.

A truly righteous person does only what's right. *All the time.*

Scripture says that though our Creator is *righteous* (Psalms 116:5; 119:7), we creatures aren't. "Not even one," the Bible flatly states (Romans 3:10).

Alas, we'd have no hope at all . . . except for the existence and arrival of "the Righteous One."

• • •

In three different New Testament sermons, leaders of the early church referred to Jesus as "the Righteous One." The apostle Peter used this phrase (it's actually one word in Greek) in Acts 3:14; the martyr Stephen in Acts 7:52; and the apostle Paul in Acts 22:14.

Its meaning is stunning: Christ was (and is) sinless. This was His own testimony—He boldly claimed that He "always" did what pleases the Father (John 8:29). And when He asked some self-righteous Pharisees, "Can any of you prove me guilty of sin?" (John 8:46).

Crickets.

(Trust me, if they could have cited even the smallest transgression, they would have.)

This claim of sinlessness was echoed by the men who knew Him best:

- Peter wrote, "He committed no sin, and no deceit was found in his mouth" (1 Peter 2:22).
- John stated, "He appeared so that he might take away our sins. And in him is no sin" (1 John 3:5).

• • •

When church people talk about "the gospel" (or good news), this is what they mean: Jesus Christ is the Righteous One sent *by* God to make unrighteous people right *with* God. He was the unblemished lamb sacrificed for the sins of the world (John 1:29) . . . and who then rose from the dead! Those who trust in Christ experience absolute forgiveness, and they are clothed forevermore in *His* righteousness (2 Corinthians 5:21).

That's not all. As we live by faith, we discover Christ's fierce commitment to make us like himself. Slowly He chips away at our rough edges. Bit by bit He transforms our desires. As we "hunger and thirst for righteousness . . ." the Righteous One satisfies our new desires, transforming us with His own spotless life (Matthew 5:6).

• • •

Today, if you survey your life and mostly see unrighteous thoughts and acts, trust the Righteous One. "God made him who had no sin to be sin for us, so that in him we might become the righteousness of God" (2 Corinthians 5:21). Today, if you find wrong desires pulling you in wrong directions, call on the Righteous One. He "understands our weaknesses, for he faced all of the same testings we do, yet he did not sin" (Hebrews 4:15 NLT).

97

RETURN

To come back or come again

Jesus answered, "If I want him to remain alive until I return, what is that to you? You must follow me." (JOHN 21:22)

Between Thanksgiving and Christmas each year, many Christians start using the word *advent*. They go to *Advent* services where they light *Advent* candles. What is all this about?

Advent comes from a Latin word that means "coming." During the Christmas season Christians celebrate three breathtaking truths: (1) The historical coming of Jesus into the world, (2) the possibility of Christ coming into our lives in a fresh and powerful way in the present, and (3) the promise that at some precise moment in the future, Christ will be *coming* again.

This second coming or advent is often referred to as the *return* of Christ.

• • •

In his gospel, John described the third time the resurrected Jesus appeared to some of His disciples (see John 21). It's a fascinating, almost humorous story involving a massive catch of fish, Jesus serving up breakfast, and the Lord talking openly to Peter about past failures and future difficulties. It was when Peter tried to re-direct the conversation that Jesus mentioned, almost in passing, His return.

This wasn't the first time Jesus had spoken of returning to earth. He'd said similar things during His final week—while talking to His disciples on Mount Olivet (Matthew 24–25) and again in the upper room (John 14:3). A few weeks after all this, when Jesus ascended straight into heaven, two angels said to His wide-eyed followers, "Men of Galilee . . . why do you stand here looking into the sky? This same Jesus, who has been taken from you into heaven, will come back in the same way you have seen him go into heaven" (Acts 1:11).

• • •

Bible passages that refer to Christ's return are the subject of intense and endless debate. Scholars, preachers, and everyday believers wrestle with how to interpret these texts and—using words like *tribulation* and *rapture*, *millennium* and *eschatology*—wrangle over the possible timing and sequence of all these future events.

Some are convinced, on the basis of current world events, that we are in the last days—as in, Christ will likely return in the next few years. Others point to Bible verses in which Jesus says, "I am coming soon" (Revelation 3:11) or the apostles' claim, "the Lord's coming is near" (James 5:8), and note that those sentences were written some two thousand years ago.

Christians may disagree about the details, but all believe Jesus *will* return. He is coming back.

• • •

It's because we *don't* know exactly when Jesus is coming that so many Bible passages urge us to be watchful and alert (Matthew 24:42–51; 25:1–30; Mark 13:24–37; 1 Thessalonians 5:1–11; 1 John 2:28).

More than charts and timelines, we need hearts that love Jesus, anticipate His coming, and long to see others come to know Him.

98

WAIT

To remain in place with expectancy about a future event

... and to wait for his Son from heaven, whom he raised from the dead—
Jesus, who rescues us from the coming wrath. (1 THESSALONIANS 1:10)

Ever stop to think how much of your life you spend waiting? A 2012 Timex survey put the figures at 20 minutes per day in traffic (presumably sitting still at stop lights), roughly 32 minutes every time we go see the doctor, and 15 minutes (on average) waiting for a table at a (non-fast-food) restaurant.

Waiting is the way of the world. Waiting is what we do . . . for the coffee to brew, for the apology, for the kids to gather up their stuff and get in the car. We wait for the train (or bus or flight), for the game to start, for a coworker to get us the information, for the offer or counteroffer. We wait for the wreck to clear, for the sequel to come out, for the mail to come, for the other shoe to drop.

Waiting is inevitable. A sour attitude while we're waiting isn't.

• • •

Multiple passages in the New Testament speak about believers *waiting* for the return of Christ. The writers use an assortment of words to convey this idea. The verb used by Paul in 1 Thessalonians 1:10 suggests waiting with patience and trust, and, in fact, *all* the other words also ooze with anticipation, not frustration.

That's the idea in the Old Testament too. Often the translators translated the same word as either "wait" or "hope." But not hope the way we typically think of it—as in crossing your fingers and engaging in wishful thinking. No, biblical hope is confident expectation. Instead of tapping your foot and complaining about the fact that nothing seems to be happening, biblical waiting is quietly reveling in what's surely coming. We replace dissatisfied grumbling with a kind of low-grade excitement.

● ● ●

The New Testament reveals that Christians have been looking expectantly for the return of Christ since the first century (James 5:8). That's a lot of waiting. (You think a couple of weeks is agonizing? Try a couple *thousand years!*)

But we needn't be discouraged. When have you ever known Jesus to break a promise? He *will* come again, as He came before—at just the right time (Galatians 4:4).

And there's no need to get disgruntled. There's plenty to do while we wait. We can let all this waiting—both for Christ and for lesser things—shape us in good ways. We can grow in patience (James 5:7; Hebrews 6:15), thankfulness (1 Thessalonians 5:17–18), and faith (Hebrews 6:12).

● ● ●

When UPS or FedEx or the USPS tells us that our package is "out for delivery" and due to arrive at any time, what do most folks do? They keep one ear open for the distinctive sound of a truck coming up the street. And if and when they think they hear that sound, they peek through the blinds eagerly.

Why? They're *waiting*.

Perhaps our waiting for the return of Christ should look a little bit more like that.

99

JUDGE

One authorized to dispense justice by punishing
the guilty and rewarding the innocent

And he ordered us to preach everywhere and to testify that Jesus is the
one appointed by God to be the judge of all—the living and the dead.

(ACTS 10:42 NLT)

There's a "version" of Jesus increasingly popular in our time. This Jesus—perhaps we could call Him "Whatever Jesus"— is easygoing and tolerant, a "live and let live" kind of guy. If He were on Twitter, His tweets would all be along the lines of "Judge not, that you be not judged" (Matthew 7:1 ESV).

Followers of this Jesus would likely peg Him as a 9 on the Enneagram. Always friendly and adaptable, He's genial, cooperative, far too busy loving people and saying "You be you!" to ever *judge* anyone.

• • •

John's gospel says God did not send Christ into the world "to judge the world" (3:17 NASB). Then it turns around and has Jesus saying, "The Father . . . has entrusted all judgment to the Son" (5:22). Matthew has Jesus referencing a *future* day of judgment (Matthew 25:32). Peter and Paul go even further, identifying Christ as the one who will "judge the living and the dead" (2 Timothy 4:1; 1 Peter 4:5).

Jesus a judge? A *judge*, by definition, makes judgments. He or she is "judgmental." Good judges don't downplay or dismiss evil. Their rulings don't conclude with the phrase, "I can see both sides." A just judge makes impartial decisions about the rightness or wrongness of actions, the guilt or innocence of persons. In describing Jesus as the final, ultimate, perfect Judge, the Bible pictures Him separating sheep from goats, punishing evil and rewarding good (Revelation 22:12), and ultimately restoring justice to the world.

● ● ●

In light of a future day of reckoning, the gospel is wonderful, startling news: Around AD 30, the future Judge of the world allowed himself to *be judged* for the sins of the world (1 John 2:2)! After living perfectly, Jesus died sacrificially . . . and rose victoriously. Those who run to Him, hide in Him, and trust in Him are pardoned. What's more, they enter into a never-ending relationship with the triune God.

The reason believers in Jesus don't have to fear a future judgment? The Judge of the world is first and foremost their Savior.

● ● ●

Two final thoughts about Jesus as Judge: (1) We don't get to accept what we like about Jesus and discard the parts that make us squirm. The New Testament presents Jesus as both Savior *and* Judge. It's only because He's full of grace *and* truth (John 1:14) that He can tell an immoral woman the two things she most needs to hear, "I don't condemn you" *and* "Leave your life of sin" (John 8:11). And (2) judging is best left in the hands of Jesus. This *isn't* to say that Christians shouldn't be discerning, or that we should refrain from calling sin what it is. It *is* a reminder to focus more on our own faults and less on the faults of others. (By the way, if we relish the judgment of sinners more than their rescue, it's a good sign we've grabbed ahold of a Jesus every bit as false as the "Whatever Jesus" so many follow.)

100

WELL DONE!

An affirmation or commendation meaning "excellent!"

"Well done, my good servant!" his master replied. "Because you have been trustworthy in a very small matter, take charge of ten cities." (LUKE 19:17)

In the 1990s, author Gary Chapman popularized the concept of "love languages"—the idea that we both express and experience love in one of five primary ways: through words of affirmation, gifts, acts of service, quality time, and physical touch. Chapman went on to argue—persuasively—that the Bible shows God speaking all these languages to His children.

In one of Jesus's best-known parables, we see the power of words of affirmation. This intriguing story features a servant who has been extremely responsible in the king's absence, and who hears the pleased monarch exclaim, "Well done, my good servant!"

• • •

Our two-word English phrase "well done" is the translation of a single word in the Greek New Testament—the adverb *euge*—which means excellent or good. We sometimes hear Brits say, "Well done, you!" We Americans are more likely to say, "Great job!" or "Excellent work!" or "Way to go!" All of these are ways of affirming or praising people for their diligent effort.

• • •

Most scholars agree that this parable of Jesus is a not-so-veiled picture of Christ's certain return and, some say, the "performance evaluation" every Christian will face when He does. Passages like 2 Corinthians 5:10 and Romans 14:10 suggest we will each be required to give an account to the Lord for how we've lived, for how well we've managed the blessings and resources He has entrusted to us in this life. This "job review" isn't for the purpose of deciding one's eternal *destiny* (that's settled when we trust in Christ); it's for determining one's eternal *opportunity*.

• • •

It's sobering to realize that in that same parable where the faithful servant hears the heart-stirring words, "Well done!" another is addressed in a very different way—as a "wicked servant" (Luke 19:22), because of his carelessness and unfaithfulness.

The teaching of the New Testament is that loyal service to God here-and-now will somehow mean greater chances for service there-and-then. So, to borrow the apostle Paul's words, "Make it your goal to please him" (2 Corinthians 5:9). Live in such a way that one day you'll hear Christ speak the ultimate words of affirmation over your life: "Well done, my good servant!"

101

LOVE

The unconditional, sacrificial commitment
to seek the best for others

As the Father has loved me, so have I loved you.
Now remain in my love. (JOHN 15:9)

A kids' choir is singing the old classic "Jesus Loves Me."
On the fourth row Michelle can hardly see the stage. Why the waterworks? Is it their sweet voices? A memory from her own tumultuous childhood? The truth of this simple, beautiful song washing over her not-always-so-pretty life?

Suffice it to say, of all the words said by Jesus and spoken (or sung) about Him, *love* tops them all.

• • •

Like so many biblical words, *love* is better depicted than defined.

So instead of propositional statements about it—"The love of God is intentional, sacrificial, unconditional, and eternal; it's the fierce and faithful commitment to seek the good of another"—how about some quick snapshots of it?

Like the time someone ran up to Jesus and breathlessly asked, "How can I earn a place in heaven?" Onlookers remembered later the way Jesus looked at this wealthy, confused young man with genuine love (Mark 10:21).

Or the time the apostle John began relating a story about a group of siblings and felt compelled to interject, "Now Jesus *loved* Martha and her sister and Lazarus" (John 11:5; emphasis added).

Or that last strange night together: The Lord playing the role of a slave and washing the feet of His followers; a Passover celebration punctuated by somber predictions of betrayal, denial, and death. Then that startling statement by Jesus to the effect of, "I want you to know I love you guys as much as the Father in heaven loves me. Don't ever forget—or walk away from—that truth" (John 15:9).

Or how about John himself? Because of his hotheaded, vengeful nature, Jesus had previously tagged John and his brother James with the nickname Sons of Thunder.* Yet by the time John wrote his gospel, he was a different man. He hinted (not so subtly) at the reason why, referring repeatedly to himself as "the disciple whom Jesus loved" (John 19:26; 20:2; 21:7, 20).

• • •

Paul of Tarsus was another whose life was transformed by the love of Jesus. While writing to Christians living in Ephesus, Paul was so overcome he fell to his knees. He prayed that Christ would make His home in their hearts as they trusted in Him. "And," he continued, "I pray that you, being rooted and established in love, may have power, together with all the Lord's holy people, to grasp how wide and long and high and deep is the love of Christ, and to know this love that surpasses knowledge" (Ephesians 3:17–19).

• • •

Can you imagine a life like that? Rooted in the "wide and long and high and deep" love of Christ! Paul says this love is far too vast

---

* See Mark 3:17 and Luke 9:51–56.

to grasp (but we should try to grab it anyway). It's much too mysterious and marvelous for us to understand (but we should pray for the grace to comprehend it anyway).

The more convinced you are that "Jesus loves me," or that you are a "disciple whom Jesus loves," the more fearless you'll be . . . and the more you'll love the way Jesus loved.

Can you think of anything you or the world need more?

DISCUSSION QUESTIONS

Suggested questions for book clubs

1. Why are words so important? (For fun, take a minute to try to describe a wordless world.)

2. What words would your peers, coworkers, neighbors, or family members use to describe Jesus of Nazareth? What five words do *you* think best describe Him?

3. Why do you suppose the apostle John, in addition to recording many of the spoken words of Jesus, actually called Jesus "*the* Word" (see John 1)? What does that name or title mean?

4. At the end of his gospel, John wrote, "Jesus did many other things as well. If every one of them were written down, I suppose that even the whole world would not have room for the books that would be written" (John 21:25). What was he suggesting by this?

5. In these pages, which words *of* Jesus or words *about* Jesus, if any,
   ___ Confused you?
   ___ Made you angry?
   ___ Helped you understand something you'd never quite grasped before?
   ___ Caused you to rethink some of your beliefs?
   ___ Encouraged you?

6. Do you have a favorite entry? Why do you think the discussion of that particular word resonated with you like it did?

7. Did this book change how you view Jesus, and if so, how?

8. What are one or two specific or practical takeaways for you from this book?

Suggested questions for small groups, Sunday school classes, or friends going through the book together

Note: *We suggest individuals read an entry a day on their own, then meet together weekly or every other week to discuss what they've read in the previous seven or fourteen days.*

1. Virgin

Why do you think Matthew and Luke made a point of asserting that Jesus was not conceived via normal, natural, biological means?

2. Immanuel

What does *Immanuel* mean, and why should this word both thrill and comfort us?

3. Born

If you'd been there for the actual birth of Jesus, what do you think you would have seen?

4. Angel

What are some wrong ideas people believe about angels?

5. Savior

People of faith hear the words *Savior* and *salvation* and immediately think of God's *ultimate* rescue from sin's penalty, from punishment in the life to come. But what are some other things God wants to deliver His people from, here and now?

6. Image

What did the apostle Paul mean when he wrote that Jesus "is the image of the invisible God" (Colossians 1:15)?

7. Magi

What misconceptions do people have about the wise men?

What do you admire most about these Persian astrologers?

8. Man

Why does it matter that Jesus was not just humanlike, but actually, fully human?

How would you answer someone who argued, "Jesus only appeared to be human"?

9. Carpenter

What do you think about the claim that Jesus spent the largest chunk of His earthly life not preaching or doing miracles but building things?

What does Jesus's work as a common carpenter say about the dignity of work?

10. Appearance

What do you imagine Jesus looked like?

Why do you think the Bible doesn't include a detailed description of Jesus's appearance?

11. Devil

How would you summarize (for a third grader) the biblical teaching about the devil?

12. It is written

What are some practical reasons it's wise to have a good grasp on God's Word?

13. Lamb

Why is it significant that John the Baptist labeled Jesus "the Lamb of God"?

14. Messiah

Test time! What would you say to a friend who asked, What does the word Messiah mean?

15. Prophet

Can you articulate why Jesus was a prophet . . . and why He was much more than a prophet?

16. Preach

What style of preaching do you prefer? Not prefer? Why?

17. Gospel

What does the gospel of Jesus mean to you?

If gospel means good news, and we naturally, instinctively share good news . . . why are so many believers so tight-lipped about the good news of Jesus?

18. Repent

What do most people think repent means? What does it actually mean?

19. Believe

How can anyone know the difference between genuine belief and defective faith?

20. Come

What did Jesus mean in the Gospels when He urged people to come to Him?

What does coming to Jesus look like in our time?

21. Called

What does the word call mean in the Bible?

What does it mean to be called by God?

22. Follow

How was "following" in the time of Christ different from what it means to "follow" today?

23. Disciples

What exactly is a disciple? (No churchy answers, please!)

24. With

What's so great about the preposition with in the Bible?

25. Kingdom

Jesus talked often about the "kingdom of God" and the "kingdom of heaven." What did He mean?

What did Jesus mean when He instructed His followers to pray, "Your kingdom come"?

26. Crowds

What's your best (and worst) experience with crowds?

Why do you think Jesus always seemed to draw a crowd?

27. Compassion

Who's the most compassionate person you know?

On a scale of 1 to 10, with 1 meaning "I'm heartless" and 10 meaning "I cry when a stranger breaks a fingernail," how compassionate are you?

28. Tired

Why do you think so many people in our culture are so tired . . . and, at the same time, so reluctant to rest?

29. Teacher

What do you think it was like to hear Jesus teach live and in person?

30. Question

What question of Jesus do you wrestle with most? Why do you think that is?

31. Parable

What's a parable?

What's your favorite Jesus parable?

32. Lord

Here's a tough one: If people had a video of the last forty-eight hours of your life, would they conclude after watching it, "Clearly, Jesus is the Lord of [your name here]"?

33. Stooped

In what way(s) is the word stooped a perfect description of Jesus?

34. Blind

In what ways is blindness both a reality and a metaphor in the Bible?

35. Poor

How would you summarize Jesus's teaching about poverty? His treatment of the poor?

What does it mean to be spiritually poor?

36. Women

In what ways was Jesus revolutionary in His attitudes toward and treatment of women?

37. Children

The Gospels show Jesus being enamored with children. Why do you think He was?

38. Sinner

What strikes you about the way Jesus interacted with sinners (irreligious people considered far from God)?

39. Heart

What does Jesus mean when He talks about our hearts?

40. Saw

Why is the common gospel phrase "Jesus saw" such an important idea?

41. Ready

What does a common boat in the Gospels teach us about serving Jesus?

42. Amazed

How were people amazed by Jesus?

How did certain people in the Gospels amaze Jesus?

43. Faith

Is faith something we have…or something we exercise? Is it a human choice … or a divine gift? Why?

44. Sabbath

For most of your life, when you've heard the word Sabbath, what thoughts have come to mind?

How, if at all, did this chapter change your views?

45. Temple

What do you think about the idea that instead of holy places, God dwells in the holy person of Jesus (and in His followers)?

46. Pharisees

How would you describe the Pharisees?

Do they deserve the bad reputation they have?

47. Pray

In what ways does the prayer life of Jesus challenge your own ideas about what it means and looks like to pray?

48. Sin

How would you describe the concept of sin to a child? To an agnostic coworker?

49. Free

Talk about a time when you felt truly free.

50. Bent over

What is something that is crippling you (emotionally, spiritually)? Where is your life "bent over" or locked up?

51. Seek

What does it say about God that He would send Jesus on a life-and-death mission to seek and save sinners?

52. Sign

What was the purpose behind all those miracles and signs Jesus did in the Gospels?

53. Fish

Do you like to fish?

What strikes you about all the references to fish in the life of Jesus?

54. Bread

Let's say the bread police inform you that you can only eat one type of bread for the rest of your life. What kind of bread would you choose?

What did Jesus mean by calling himself "the bread of life"?

55. Gate

What's the significance of Jesus referring to himself as the narrow gate?

56. Get up

In what specific area of your life do you need to obey Jesus's command to "get up"?

57. Hell

How do you understand the teaching of Jesus about hell?

58. Heaven

What are some of your beliefs about heaven—and where in the Bible do you see those ideas?

59. Church

In your experience, what do you love about church?

What would you change about your church if you could?

60. Forgiven

What does it feel like to be forgiven?

What's the hardest thing about letting someone else off the hook?

61. Touch

Are you a touchy, huggy, affectionate person? Or does too much touching make you uncomfortable?

When, if ever, have you felt like Jesus touched you?

62. Serve

Why is serving others so hard?

63. Fulfill

How does Jesus fulfill all God's ancient promises about a coming Messiah?

64. Transfigured

What do you think was the purpose of Jesus's transfiguration?

65. Listen

If someone polled the twenty-five people who know you best, what collective grade would they give you when it comes to listening?

How well do you listen for God's voice as you go about your daily tasks?

66. Wept

When's the last time you bawled your eyes out? Or if you can't remember back that far, what things in life tend to get you choked up or misty-eyed?

Does it attract or repel you to know that Jesus sometimes cried?

67. Truly

Why did Jesus say the word truly so much?

68. Whoever

Why is the word whoever one of the most beautiful words Jesus ever said?

69. Give

If you could give anyone any gift, what would you give? To whom and why?

70. Remain

What did Jesus mean when He told His followers to "remain in me" (John 15:4)?

71. In

What does it mean to be "in" Christ?

72. Shepherd

Have you ever seen a shepherd in action? What do you know about that occupation, and why is it an apt description of Jesus?

73. Joy

What's your reaction to Jesus's prayer that His followers might be filled with joy (John 17:13)?

On most days, would joyful be a word that others use to describe you? Why or why not?

74. Peace

In your relationship with God, where are on you on the following peace scale?

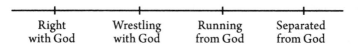

| Right with God | Wrestling with God | Running from God | Separated from God |

75. Grace

When in your life have you had the greatest experience of the grace of Jesus?

76. Truth

What does it mean when Jesus says He is the truth?

77. Hypocrite

Why was Jesus so angered by hypocrisy?

78. Woe

What are some things Jesus might say "Woe!" about if He came to your town, your house, or your workplace today?

79. Light

Why is light such a great spiritual metaphor?

Where in your life could you use a little spiritual light?

80. Life

Where in your experience (emotions, relationships, situations, etc.) do you need Jesus to inject some life?

81. Zacchaeus

Do you agree that Zacchaeus is, in certain ways, representative of all people? Why or why not?

82. Hated

Jesus warned His followers on multiple occasions that they would be hated. Given that fact, why do you think modern (Western) Christians get so outraged and indignant when secular people and irreligious cultures mock and scorn their faith?

83. Hosanna

What does Hosanna mean, and why is it a great word?

84. Spit

What do you make of all the references to "spit" in the life of Jesus?

85. Crucified

When Jesus was crucified, only some of His followers stuck around. Do you think you would have? Why or why not?

86. Inscription

What was ironic about the inscription Pilate ordered his men to place above the head of the crucified Jesus?

87. Clothes

What's your response to the claim of historians that Jesus was almost certainly relieved of His clothes (stripped naked) when He was nailed to the cross?

88. Curtain

What's the significance of the tearing—from top to bottom—of the big, thick veil, or curtain, in the temple's most holy place?

89. Earthquake

Have you ever been in an earthquake? If so, what was that experience like?

What kind of positive shaking probably needs to happen in your life?

90. Garden

Why do you think garden imagery is such a prominent theme in the Bible and in the life of Jesus?

91. Risen

Why does it matter that Jesus actually, physically, literally rose from the dead?

92. Doubt

On a scale of 1 to 10, with 1 meaning "total trust" and 10 signifying "extreme doubt," where would you score yourself in the following areas:

_____ God's existence

_____ God's presence in my life

_____ God's care for me

_____ God's answering of my prayers

_____ God's forgiveness of my sins

How would you counsel a friend who confessed big struggles with doubt?

93. Apostle

What's the difference between an Apostle (capital A) and an apostle (lowercase a)?

94. Again

In what ways is the word *again* a gospel word?

95. Go

What are some places you could (and maybe should) go for Jesus?

What makes going hard or scary?

96. Righteous One

Why does it matter that Jesus is righteous?

97. Return

What are three practical ways we can show we are expecting the return of Jesus?

98. Wait

When it comes to waiting, how good of a waiter are you?

How can we make the most of the time during which we have to wait?

99. Judge

More and more, Christians are accused of being judgmental. In your opinion, is this a fair accusation?

How does it affect you to remember that one day all believers will stand before the Lord and give an account for how we have served Him?

100. Well done!

Why is receiving affirmation or commendation such a powerful thing?

101. Love

What would you tell a person who confessed, "Sometimes I have a hard time believing that Jesus would love someone like me . . . I mean, I read that idea in the Bible, but it's like I can't seem to fully accept it. I want to believe it. How can I take those words to heart?"

A graduate of Louisiana State University and Dallas Theological Seminary, Len Woods was a pastor for more than twenty-five years. He's authored or coauthored more than twenty books, most recently *101 Important Words of the Bible* and *the Unforgettable Story They Tell* (Our Daily Bread Publishing), *Spiritual Life Hacks* (Harvest House), and *The One Year Book of Best-Loved Bible Verses* (Tyndale House). Now, as a StoryBrand Certified Guide/Copywriter, he spends his days helping good businesses use clear words to find more customers to serve. You can find out more at lenwoods.com.

INDEX

Help us get the word out!

Our Daily Bread Publishing exists to feed the soul with the Word of God.

If you appreciated this book, please let others know.

- Pick up another copy to give as a gift.
- Share a link to the book or mention it on social media.
- Write a review on your blog, on a bookseller's website, or at our own site (odb.org/store).
- Recommend this book for your church, book club, or small group.

Connect with us:

- @ourdailybread
- @ourdailybread
- @ourdailybread

Our Daily Bread Publishing
PO Box 3566
Grand Rapids, Michigan 49501 USA

✉ books@odb.org